Cambridge Elements ☰

Elements in Applied Social Psychology
edited by
Susan Clayton
College of Wooster, Ohio

UNDOING THE GENDER BINARY

Charlotte Chucky Tate
San Francisco State University

Ella Ben Hagai
California State University, Fullerton

Faye J. Crosby
University of California, Santa Cruz

CAMBRIDGE
UNIVERSITY PRESS

University Printing House, Cambridge CB2 8BS, United Kingdom

One Liberty Plaza, 20th Floor, New York, NY 10006, USA

477 Williamstown Road, Port Melbourne, VIC 3207, Australia

314–321, 3rd Floor, Plot 3, Splendor Forum, Jasola District Centre, New Delhi – 110025, India

79 Anson Road, #06–04/06, Singapore 079906

Cambridge University Press is part of the University of Cambridge.

It furthers the University's mission by disseminating knowledge in the pursuit of education, learning, and research at the highest international levels of excellence.

www.cambridge.org
Information on this title: www.cambridge.org/9781108731133
DOI: 10.1017/9781108584234

© Charlotte Chucky Tate, Ella Ben Hagai, and Faye J. Crosby 2020

First published 2020

A catalogue record for this publication is available from the British Library.

ISBN 978-1-108-73113-3 Paperback
ISSN 2631-777X (online)
ISSN 2631-7761 (print)

Cambridge University Press has no responsibility for the persistence or accuracy of URLs for external or third-party internet websites referred to in this publication and does not guarantee that any content on such websites is, or will remain, accurate or appropriate.

Undoing the Gender Binary

Elements in Applied Social Psychology

DOI: 10.1017/9781108584234
First published online: May 2020

Charlotte Chucky Tate
San Francisco State University

Ella Ben Hagai
California State University, Fullerton

Faye J. Crosby
University of California, Santa Cruz

Author for correspondence: Charlotte Chucky Tate, ctate2@sfsu.edu

Abstract: The central question of this Element is this: What does it mean to be transgender – in general and in specific ways? What does the designation mean for any individual and for the groups in which the individual exists? Biologically, what occurs? Psychologically, what transpires? The Element starts with the basics. The authors question some traditional assumptions, lay out some biomedical information, and define their terms. They then move to the question of central concern, seen first in terms of the individual and then in terms of the group or society. They conclude with some implications, urging some new approaches to research and suggest some applications in the classroom and beyond.

Keywords: transgender, gender, nonbinary, transphobia

ISBNs: 9781108731133 (PB), 9781108584234 (OC)
ISSNs: 2631-777X (online), ISSN 2631-7761 (print)

Contents

1 Introduction   1

2 The Basics   5

3 The Processes of Transitioning Away from the Gender
  Assigned at Birth   14

4 Multifaceted Model of Gender   25

5 Lived Experiences of Public Figures   36

6 Social Scientific Studies of Rejection and Acceptance   48

7 Reflections and Parting Wishes   62

  References   68

1 Introduction

This is a scholarly work about "gender" and the vast array of its meanings in US society. Open-minded people who are not transgender constitute our primary audience. For at least one of the authors, who is cisgender (which we will define), the endeavor to demystify "gender" and unpack its multiple meanings is profoundly personal. A few years ago, a member of the author's family, deeply loved by the author, announced his intention to live as the gender he had felt to be his true gender even when the world saw him first as a girl and then as a woman. The author wished to understand more about the experiences of her family member but did not want to burden the family member with the task of education. She found texts like Nicholas Reich's (2012) *Transgender 101* and Anne Boedecker's (2011) *The Transgender Guidebook* that offered excellent beginnings, and these texts spoke primarily to a trans audience rather than to an audience of cisgender allies. The author was left with questions, especially about the fit between society and trans individuals. She hungered for more concepts to help guide her thinking. When the opportunity arose to join forces with the other two authors, both authorities on issues of gender identity and sexual orientation – and how they differ – the knowledge-hungry author felt joy and relief.

Yet, the project of writing a monograph is also personal and, in this case, the challenge we faced as authors was trying to coordinate the thoughts, perspectives, and voices of three very different women. We come from three very different generations (or cohorts) of academic scholarship within the same discipline (psychology), which means that our own ideas about how to introduce, discuss, and explain issues of gender are quite distinctive. Unabashedly, our perspectives come from different waves of feminist thought in the United States (even if some would disagree about whether "waves" is a useful way to discuss this) including the 1960–70s, the 1990s, and the early 2000s, in addition to trying to speak to current feminist issues (circa 2019). Consequently, the narrative voice of this monograph is not univocal; instead, the reader will hear three different voices – alternating sometimes between sentences – but those voices are directed toward a common goal. We hope that a strength of the different voices is that a broad set of readers can access this work and find their own cultural references and touchstones within the trove presented that literally spans many decades. It is in this spirit that we invite readers to bring their own experiences and find whatever usefulness they can in this work. Additionally, we focus squarely on the United States in our discussion of these issues. Two of the authors were born and raised in the United States, and all authors have conducted scholarly work (in whole or in part) in the cultural context of the

United States. Consequently, we feel most comfortable making statements about the US cultural context and not necessarily about cultures with which we have little direct experience.

Many humans classify themselves and are classified by others as either female or male. Some societies (e.g., Argentina, Denmark, India, Malta, Norway, Spain, Sweden, the United Kingdom) have gone further in their cultural expectations of what two genders could mean and that there are more than two genders. Some cultures (e.g., India, Sweden) even include third-gender pronouns that refer to people rather than the generic third-person forms of many languages. Nonetheless, when thinking about just two genders – think Adam and Eve, Romeo and Juliet, Fred and Ginger – the list of couples could go on and on. Such a list would seem natural to those who assume that humans come in two forms: men and women. Such a list also would – and often does – reinforce the assumption of the universality of the gender binary. So strong is the tendency to see the world in terms of the gender binary that the men–women division is often extended to nonhuman entities as well (Bem, 1993). Think mother earth and father sky. At first glance, the division of the world into male and female might seem to spring inevitably from the demands of sexual reproduction. Sexual reproduction, we learn from elementary textbooks, occurs when the combination of genetic information from two separate organisms or two types of organisms (i.e., the male type and the female type) results in new life. Sexual reproduction contrasts with asexual reproduction, which occurs when a single organism reproduces itself, as in mitosis. Sexual reproduction is critical for evolution, allowing as it does for novel combinations of genetic material. Upon reflection, the division between male and female becomes less universal and rigid. Some animals, like the banana slug, are hermaphroditic. Other animals, like striped bass, change their biological sex over the life span (Berlinsky & Specker, 1991). Fungi have many sexes (Raper, 1966).

The vast majority of humans self-categorize their gender in the way that is consistent with how those in authority categorized them at birth. Yet, if only one half of one percent of humans did not see themselves as entirely male or female in accord with the label given them by one or more experts, an estimated 35,000,000 people worldwide would defy the gender binary. That's more than ten times the population of Mongolia; it's four times the population of Switzerland.

Today Americans, especially those who live on either coast, seem increasingly accepting of gender fluidity (Aitken et al., 2015; Travers, 2018). But while overtly accepting of new norms, many individuals still harbor old prejudices (Goldberg & Kuvalanka, 2018; Goldberg et al., 2019). And prejudiced or not, many people acknowledge an uncomfortable lack of knowledge and a galling confusion about terminology. Many potential allies to the transgender (trans) community may fear that they create a bad impression on would-be friends through sheer ignorance about terminology and basic concepts.

The central purpose of our Element is to present the basics, clarifying terms and demystifying knowledge about people who identify as transgender. We hope to present sound scholarship in a nontechnical and inviting way. We hope that those who are not part of any trans community will gain new understandings of what is involved in living as a trans person.

Cisgender people (or cis people, for short) are those who experience their gender with the same label that they were gender assigned at birth. Transgender people (or trans people, for short) are people who experience their gender as different from their assigned gender at birth. Some, but not all, transgender people may choose to change their legal status or their physical appearance. Identification with a gender different than the one assigned by authorities is the essential component of the definition of transgender identity that we adopt in this volume.

Even though cis people constitute our primary audience, we hope that our work will prove reassuring as well as helpful to people on the transgender spectrum. We expect that some of the information contained here will be new even to those who are active in trans communities. For those who are questioning aspects of their gender identity, this work is meant to be an aid. For example, in Section 4, we present the multifaceted model of gender. Some of the conceptualizations presented there might give expression to ideas that have sought concrete form in the minds of some trans people. Even for people who have been thinking about these issues for a long time, we hope that we are providing a vocabulary for helpful discussions. We wish to allow for affirmation through concepts and information.

Our work proceeds in seven sections. After this introduction, we present basic information, defining terms and outlining the biological foundations of what is called "sex." In the third section we give basic information about different paths that can be taken when a person transitions away from the sex assigned at birth, including information about hormonal and surgical interventions. The fourth section presents the "facet model of gender." We do not claim that individuals walk around with this model in their heads any more than we name the parts of speech each time we form a sentence. Our model, developed by Charlotte Tate, provides conceptual clarity, allowing us to keep the referents of "gender" separate from each other. We turn in Section 5 to the lived experiences of those on the transgender spectrum as recounted in popular memoirs. It is through these sources that most of the public learns about transgender issues, and so we accord to them a separate part of our work. In Section 6 of our Element, we examine the attitudes of the majority toward those in the minority as documented by social scientists. Our short final Section 7 is speculative, addressing questions of both a philosophical and practical nature.

General readers may find themselves skimming over some sections of the work, especially if they have a low tolerance for technical details. And specialized readers like gender researchers may find themselves lingering over some new information while feeling quite familiar with other information. Although it is of course impossible to satisfy and intrigue all audiences all the time, we hope that our work offers a welcoming entry for many into a world of thought-provoking knowledge and ideas, and we hope that some readers will develop into the next generation of researchers and perhaps even authors on issues of gender and gender identity.

1.1 Topical and Enduring Issues

We believe that contemplation of what it means to be transgender is important not only because it allows us to understand the lived experiences of a particular demographic group. Rather, we propose that thinking about a world in which some people are transgender – whether or not you are one of those people – allows us to explore the idea of gender fluidity and to thus rethink what is gained and what is lost when we think of human beings as falling into discrete, immutable categories.

Our Element project is quite topical, but the transgender experience is quite ancient (Green, 1998). Consider the Hijra in India who appeared first in ancient Hindu texts like the Kamasutra. The Hijra community in India are understood as being a third gender. Hijra wear colorful saris and makeup. They are believed to have a spiritual power to bless or curse. The Ramayana tells the story of Rama who was banished to a forest for fourteen years. In the forest, he called to his followers telling those who were men or women to return to the city. Members of the Hijra community did not feel bound to such a call (as they did not identify as men or women), so they stayed in the forest and Rama blessed them for their loyalty. Currently, the Hijra live mostly in Mumbai; their community is hierarchical in that older Hijras take care of younger Hijras (Hylton, Gettleman, & Lyons, 2018; Michelraj, 2015). As early as the sixteenth century, two-spirit people held important roles among the Cherokee and other Native American tribes. The two-spirit category represents people who integrate feminine and masculine traits. Two-spirit identity was believed to be grounded in supernatural intervention that became known through visions or dreams. Two-spirit people were and are often healers, shamans, and ceremony leaders (Smithers, 2014).

Among other postcolonial Americans, too, history contains examples of individuals who presented as the gender not assigned to them by others. The historian Susan Stryker (2008) writes, "in the eighteenth century, numerous women and trans masculine people – most famously Deborah Sampson – enlisted in the Revolutionary Army as men" (p. 46). Transgender soldiers also participated in the American Civil War. Transgender soldiers, Albert Cashier and Harry Burford, served in the Union and the Confederate army respectively. Frances Thompson, a black slave and transgender woman, was one of the five women who testified in front of Congress regarding the brutal rapes that occurred during the 1866 Memphis Riots (Stryker, 2008).

Although some people have defied the gender binary across the millennia, it is only in recent times that transgender individuals are not singled out as belonging to some defined and separate form of humanity. It is only now that individuals in the mainstream of society are not certain to be stigmatized for defying the impulse toward the gender binary. We believe that twenty years ago, a review like ours would likely not have existed. And thus we see this work as wholly contemporary.

There is another way in which this Element shows a timestamp. We expect and hope that many parts of our volume will be out-of-date within a decade or two. Medical realities will change. The current medical thinking, for example, is that puberty-arresting drugs have few negative side effects, and so are helpful for youth who are not sure if they wish to transition; but continued study over time may change that opinion. Attitudes will evolve. As more and more people feel it is safe to express their identities, gender nonconformity will become less controversial; and that in turn may make it seem even safer to even more people to eschew rigid gender roles. As realities change, scholarly understandings will, of necessity, shift.

Even as we embrace the topical nature of our work, we also hope that the information presented here will do more than contribute to how readers see a specific current issue. We would like to imagine that readers will be sparked to reflect on enduring realities. How privileged we are to be able to pause and contemplate eternal questions of what it means to be female, what it means to be male, what it means to be nonbinary, and ultimately what it means to be human.

2 The Basics

2.1 Terms

Let's start by defining some terms. We do this for expository clarity but not to dictate that all other researchers use exactly the same terms as we do. We recognize that there have been some scholarly battles over evolving terminology (American Psychological Association, 2015; Crawford & Fox, 2007). But, like Teich (2012), a social worker with a distinctly compassionate approach to scholarship, we think that some discussion of key terms will help with an understanding of more complex concepts.

In many instances, the terms *sex* and *gender* are used interchangeably, but usually, we use the term *sex to* refer to the anatomical features that are commonly used to classify humans into female and male. *Assigned or birth sex* is the classification that adults – including adult authorities like physicians – use when they classify human babies as female or male. The assignment is generally made on the basis of external genitalia. On an average of one birth per two thousand live births, the genitalia are ambiguous. In such cases, the child might be called *intersex*, but sooner or later, authorities may push the child toward one designation or the other.

When an individual has the same label as their birth-sex throughout life, that individual is said to be *cisgender* because *cis* is Latin for "on the same side as." Individuals who were assigned to the category of female at birth and who continue to experience themselves as female become, as adults, *cis women*. Individuals who were assigned to the category of male at birth and who continue to experience themselves as male become, as adults, *cis men*.

Not all individuals continue to experience themselves as being the sex assigned to them at birth. Such individuals, we call *transgender* (or *trans* for short). In our definition, a *trans woman* (adult) or *trans girl* (child) is any woman or girl who was assigned to the category male at birth (almost always based on external genitals) and who nonetheless experiences gender category as female. Likewise, in our definition, a *trans man* (adult) or *trans boy* (child) is any man or boy who was assigned to the category female at birth (almost always based on external genitals) and who nonetheless experiences his gender category as male.

It should be noted that our definition of transgender is not the first or only that exists in scholarly literature. One of the better-known definitions of transgender is presented by Stryker (2008). Stryker defines transgender broadly, using the concept of the transgender umbrella (also, American Psychological Association, 2015; Williams, 2014). She uses the term "transgender umbrella" to:

> refer to people who move away from the gender they were assigned at birth, people who cross over (*trans-*) the boundaries constructed by their culture to define and contain that gender because they feel strongly that they properly belong to another gender in which it would be better for them to live; others want to strike out toward some new location, some space not yet clearly defined or concretely occupied; still others simply feel the need

to get away from the conventional expectations bound up with the gender that was initially put upon them. In any case, it is the *movement across a socially imposed boundary away from an unchosen starting place* – rather than any particular destination or mode of transition – that best characterizes the concept of "transgender" that I want to develop here. (p. 1; italics in original)

Stryker's definition includes many experiences from changing one's legal designation, to behaving in ways described as gender nonconforming. Our definition is much more targeted because we only focus on the birth-assigned and self-assigned labels for oneself – not behaviors consistent or inconsistent with gender stereotypes or gender conformity.

Focusing on birth-assigned and self-assigned labels also allows us to include those whose self-assigned gender identity labels are not exclusively female or male. For example, there are people who identify as *agender* – being neither female nor male – irrespective of their assigned sex category. There are also people who identify as *genderfluid, genderblended, or androgynous* – being both female and male, either concurrently or alternately – and other specific labels, that differ from their assigned sex. These specific labels of agender and genderblended fit into a larger class of experiences that other scholars have labeled *genderqueer* –with queer meaning unexpected or unusual, or not fitting within the gender binary (e.g., Nestle, Howell, & Wilchins, 2002). Currently, scholars also use the label *nonbinary* to indicate people who do not think of themselves as exclusively one of the familiar two categories (e.g., Galupo, Pulice-Farrow, & Ramirez, 2019; Hyde et al., 2019; Tate, Youssef, & Bettergarcia, 2014).

Trans individuals are, by definition, unable to be complacent about issues of sex and gender in a society that is so interested in a very particular form of the binary in which everyone is expected to be cisgender. Because assigned genders almost always convey expectations about how one should act, to whom one should feel attracted, and with whom one should have sexual contact, gay and bisexual people also generally find complacency out of their reach. It seems natural, therefore, that trans and gay people have sought a common cause in resisting prejudice and discrimination. Organizations often use the phrases LGBT (lesbian, bisexual, gay, and transgender) or LBGTQ (adding queer) or LBGTQIA+ (adding other sexual orientations and gender identities, as well as other sexual and gender identities with the +).

Although solidarity among sexual and gender minorities is politically and socially helpful, phrases like LGBT can introduce confusion among people who are not centrally involved in the issues. The phrase LGBT confounds gender identity and sexual orientation.

Yet, self-assigned gender is not the same as *sexual orientation* or *sexual preference*. How one thinks of oneself – as female or male or neither or both – that is, one's own identity, is connected to but different from one's attraction to sexual, romantic, or affectional partners. For example, some trans women (i.e., individuals who were assigned to the category of a male at birth and who think of themselves as women) might have sexual partners who are exclusively men; other trans women have sexual partners who are exclusively women; still other trans women have sexual partners who are men and women; still other trans women do not have sexual partners because they are not sexually attracted to other people. The same would apply to a trans man. Stated another way, any trans woman might be a lesbian, straight, bisexual, or asexual, just as a trans man might be a gay man, straight, bisexual, or asexual. Of course, the same applies to any cis woman or cis man. We will return to this issue in the next section, but one simple way to keep the concepts clear is to remember that sexual orientation (straight, bi, gay) refers to whom you would like to go to bed *with* while gender identity (cis, trans) refers to who you go to bed *as*.

2.2 Biological Bases of Gender

Think of a time when one of your friends returned from a special trip and you asked about the people living in the destination. Perhaps your friend replied saying, "Well, fundamentally, people are just people." Perhaps you nodded, agreeing about the universality of humanity.

Notice how different is the assumption of universality from the prejudgment that humans are fundamentally different from each other in profound ways. The profoundly different view of people held sway in the 1980s, 1990s, and early 2000s. For instance, Carol Gilligan's (1982) book, *In a Different Voice*, enjoyed huge success in academic circles, purporting to show that women have an ethic of care while men have an ethic of justice. Outside the academy, popularizers like John Gray (2009) gained currency with the catch phrase: "Men are from Mars, women are from Venus."

Those who emphasize gender dimorphism, who see females and males as fundamentally distinct life-forms, might be surprised to learn that biological sex is a multidimensional concept. Researchers usually identify four components that are thought to make up the primary sex characteristics: chromosomes, external genitalia, internal genitalia, and hormones (Crawford, 2006). Some authors also differentiate between prenatal or uterine hormones, on the one hand, and, on the other, postnatal hormones.

2.2.1 Multidimensional Nature of Biological Sex

The multidimensional nature of biological sex means that gender categories are less black-and-white than envisioned by authors like Gilligan and Gray. Primary sex characteristics usually, but not always, align with individuals' gender identity, behavior, and/or presentation. And to complicate matters even more, the dimensions are just that: dimensional – existing along a continuum.

We suspect that a portion of the discomfort that some people feel about trans people springs from a sense of dissonance and unease that can arise by confronting the errors of "a truth" that we – as a society – have taken as foundational. Just as ancient theologians assumed that the sun rotated around the earth, so do many of us assume that gender or biological sex is uncomplicated, being immutable and unidimensional. In fact, gender is neither immutable nor unidimensional. But while it is simply false to imagine that all humans come in one of two clear, absolutely distinct, and unchanging varieties (male and female), it can also be unsettling to recognize the problems of our prior conceptualizations. Galileo was no hero to many of his contemporaries not only because his calculations were hard to conceive, but also because his new conceptualization of the heavens challenged old truths taken to be sacred and self-evident.

Chromosomes. You can start with chromosomes. Many people believe that assigned sex is controlled entirely by sex chromosomes, which are commonly depicted as X or Y based on how they look when magnified under a microscope. The common belief is that an XX chromosomal pair will always lead to the assigned sex of female and that an XY chromosomal pair will always lead to the assigned sex of male.

Reality is more complex. To begin, there are many sex chromosome configurations in addition to XX and XY. In fact, there are six major chromosomal configurations for humans: (1) XX, (2) XY, (3) X0 (i.e., a single X-chromosome without a partner), (4) XXY, (5) XYY, and (6) XXX (Blackless et al., 2000). In addition to those, there are the even less common configurations of XXYY (Nielsen & Wohlert, 1991), XXXY, and XXXXY (Kleczkowska, Fryns, & Van den Berghe, 1988). It is clear that some chromosomal configurations affect bodily morphology – that is, how the body looks during development. For instance, X0 (also called Turner's Syndrome) has a characteristic lack of development of the secondary sex characteristics, specifically the chest area. Although individuals with an X0 configuration have vaginal and vulval genital structures, they do not develop the fatty tissue and contours around the chest area that are described as adult breasts (e.g., Gravholt et al., 1998). In parallel, those people with XXY configurations (also called Klinefelter's Syndrome) often have adult breasts and a penile scrotal structure (e.g., Kruse et al., 1998).

While morphological effects of chromosomal configurations are apparent, psychological outcomes are less understood. But for one perspective, reviewing much of the literature to that point, Hines (2005) has argued that the psychology associated with gender identity may have more to do with prenatal hormones – uptake and/or insensitivity to androgens in particular – than chromosomal configurations as such. Part of her argumentation can be seen by the fact that there are some adult women (who have vaginal and vulval structures from birth) who have XY chromosomal configurations based on being insensitive to the update of androgens prenatally (Hines, 2005).

Hormones. Each chromosome in the configuration (whether a singleton, a pair, a trio, or larger) signals the releases of classes of specific hormones collected into the general names of androgens and estrogens. While androgens (e.g., testosterone, dihydrotestosterone) are sometimes called the "male" hormones and estrogens (e.g., progesterone, estriol) the "female" hormones, all sex chromosomes produce some amount of both of these classes. Thus, everyone has "female" and "male" hormones even before birth.

What usually differentiates around the eighth week of gestation into a female configuration (with a vulva and vagina) or a male configuration (with a penis and scrotum) starts out as one mass of undifferentiated genital materials. These are shown in Figure 1. By the twelfth week of in utero gestation, the [internal or external] genitals have usually reached their prenatal maturation state.

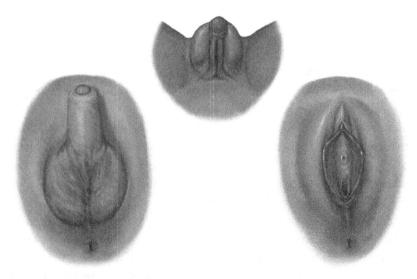

Figure 1 Initial genital material for humans and fully developed genital divergence around twelfth week of fetal development

Genitalia. Generally, the newborn has one of these two genital configurations. We should think of the component parts (e.g., the clitoris or the glans) as parallel structures, as seen in Figure 2, having emerged from undifferentiated tissue shown in Figure 1. On rare occasions, the external genitalia are ambiguous. Human genital development is a difference of degree, not kind, and controlled by androgen uptake in utero – not directly by sex chromosomes. This means that any person with an XX pair of sex chromosomes could have any of the genital forms from vulva/vagina to penis/scrotum (Dessens, Slijper, & Drop, 2005; Hines, 2005; Hines, Brook, & Conway, 2004). Likewise, a person with a pair of XY chromosomes could have any of the genital forms, including a vulva/vagina form. Current thinking sees the female configuration as the default option, with the vulva and vagina forming from the undifferentiated genital tissue prior to the penis and scrotum. Our current understanding of intersex genital conditions is that they are largely the consequence of releasing either too little or too much intra-utero androgen, or, separately, the body either being insensitive to the uptake of androgens or being overly sensitive to them (Rodriguez-Buritica, 2015).

It is worth noting that when babies are born in the United States and other industrialized nations, obstetricians rarely conduct DNA tests to understand sex chromosomes, measure hormone tests to determine androgen levels or androgen receptivity, or look at the internal genitalia. Instead, pediatricians look at the form of the newborn's genitals and make a designation of whether the baby should be assigned to the category of female (based on the clear presence of vulva/vagina forms) or male (based on the clear presence of penis/scrotum forms).

When the genital form is not so clear, obstetricians rely on a Prader scale (see Figure 2) to determine how close to either the vulva/vagina form or the penis/scrotum form the genitals are to determine which type of surgery should be performed to make these intersex genitals appear more like one of the two prototypical forms.

The story does not stop with the external genitalia. Sometimes the internal genitalia do not correspond to the external genitalia. In what is called Turner Syndrome, an individual has a single X chromosome, resulting in forty-five (rather than forty-six) chromosomes. Turner's Syndrome is often depicted as X0. Most individuals with the X0 configuration develop a vagina and vulva at birth – external genitalia – but their internal genitalia, specifically the uterus, is underdeveloped biologically speaking and often remains so after the rush of pubertal hormones (Morgan, 2007). Consequently, many medical professionals believe that in order for the internal genitalia to develop in-utero and continue at puberty, an individual needs at least two sex chromosomes (cf. Morgan, 2007).

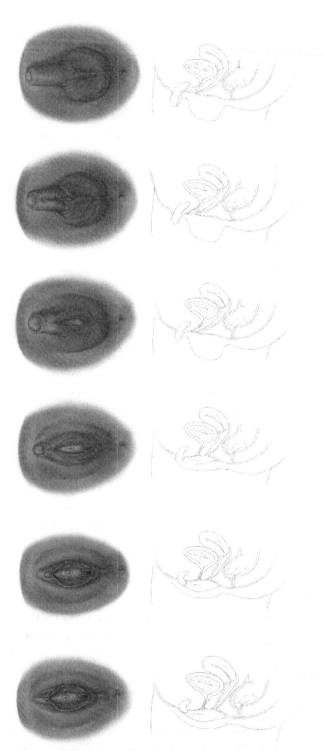

Figure 2 The Prader scale for determining assigned sex at birth for intersex conditions

Internal and external genitalia can develop differently for other reasons as well. Medical professionals have identified several forms of what is called androgen insensitivity (Mazur, 2005; Zuloaga et al., 2008). This insensitivity to androgens can happen in-utero during the differentiation of genital development and also persist into puberty. A consistent feature of androgen insensitivity is that the internal structures are usually undifferentiated as either testes or ovaries. Because of this, if the individual is assigned female at birth, people can be surprised when menstruation does not occur during puberty (Gurney & Simmonds, 2007).

In another medical condition called dihydrotestosterone (DHT)-deficiency (or more formally "5-alpha-reductase deficiency"), people appear to have vulva and vaginal structures at birth, but, during puberty, testicles descend into the labia majora (the outer lips, which are the same biological material as the scrotum) and a penile shaft emerges (which is the same biological material as the clitoris and the vaginal canal) (Cohen-Kettenis, 2005; Imperato-McGinley et al., 1979). Clearly, biological processes are more varied and intricate than is commonly presented in popular discussions of biology when it comes to both sex and gender.

Secondary Sex Characteristics. While only four components are generally thought to make up the primary sex characteristics, there are additional components that comprise the secondary sex characteristics. Secondary sex characteristics are not always defined in the same way by human biologists, human anatomists, and medical professionals. Some scholars emphasize what is called "vital capacity," which is the volume of air held by the lungs. Other aspects of anatomy that are commonly seen as "secondary sex characteristics" include center of gravity, leg length at any given height, facial shape, vocal depth, and shoulder and hip movement when locomoting. However, there is near universal agreement across disciplines on three secondary sex characteristics: (1) breast size and shape, (2) muscle-to-fat ratio, and (3) body hair coverage and thickness, including facial hair. Interestingly, during childhood, none of the three secondary sex characteristics differentiates females from males. Children do not differ much in their chest size, muscle-to-fat ratios (without intensive exercise), or their body hair coverage and thickness.

During puberty, with the onslaught of estrogens and androgens in different quantities, humans appear increasingly dimorphic in terms of secondary sex characteristics. "Secondary" literally signals that the changes happen second in a time sequence – at puberty and not at or before birth. Those assigned female at birth tend to show growth in breast size and shape (e.g., sometimes initially called "breast budding") that far outpaces the growth of the same tissue in those assigned male at birth. Breast development is based largely on the action of estrogens. Similarly, and related to the development of comparatively larger breast tissue as increased adipose (or fat), the muscle-to-fat ratio tends to be more equal for those assigned female at birth. This muscle-to-fat ratio is again attributable to the action of estrogens increasing body fat in certain areas (e.g., breasts, hips, buttocks). On the flipside of this same phenomenon, those assigned male at birth tend to have a higher muscle-to-fat ratio; remember, however, this is a distribution – meaning that some may have a ratio of muscle-to-fat that is lower than that of some who are categorized as female. The muscle mass increase is based largely on the action of androgens.

Finally, during puberty, those labeled male at birth tend to increase their body hair coverage and thickness at a level that far outpaces the same action in those assigned female at birth. (Notice that everyone has an increase in body hair coverage and thickness; the statement is comparative. The more direct way to understand this is to notice the genital hair coverage and thickness being similar in all people at puberty, irrespective of their birth-assigned category). The body hair coverage and thickness are largely based on the action of testosterone. Thus, adult cis men tend to enjoy more and thicker body hair and facial hair than adult cis women do; but, remember that there are social factors at play too, including consistent hair removal for many adult cis women on areas of their bodies, especially the face.

3 The Processes of Transitioning Away from the Gender Assigned at Birth

It is difficult to get reliable information about some of the basic questions that people might have about transgender experience because much of the medical and psychological literature is either incomplete or has not focused on certain topics. For instance, the fourth edition of the Diagnostic and Statistical Manual of Mental Disorders (DSM-IV; APA 2014) has estimated the prevalence of trans women in the United States to be 12,000–14,000 persons. The estimated prevalence of trans men was a smaller number. However, both estimates are based on only those who sought and received genital reassignment surgeries. Consequently, those trans women and men who did not receive surgeries are missing from this count. Furthermore, before the 20-teens, genital surgeries for trans men seem to have been less prevalent based on the techniques available before that time, making the count for trans men necessarily lower than that for trans women. Additionally, the DSM-IV did not count genderqueer or nonbinary trans individuals – that is, those trans persons who do not consistently or exclusively identify as women or men. When nonbinary persons are included in research both past and present, the samples have been small (e.g., Factor &

Rothblum, 2008) and have been largely used for qualitative analysis on questions about lived experiences (e.g., Galupo et al., 2019) – not for population-based estimates.

Similarly, because the focus has been on trans women and men and those who have received genital surgeries, it is extremely difficult to provide good answers to basic quantitative questions, such as: What are the average (mean) and most frequent (modal) ages of transitioning? Even an age-focused question is complicated by access to medical services that varies with ethnicity and socio-economic class in the United States and many other societies. Likewise, since surgery tends to be the main record-keeping focus, it is difficult to determine the actual incidence of trans people who retain their trans identity over time – because this would, at best, be limited to those individuals who received surgery (and follow-up post surgery).

If there is any consensus about studying transgender people, it is that the ultimate cause is currently unknown. Of course, each scientific discipline with human behavior as a focus has its own hypotheses and predictable starting points. Genetics researchers point science toward the possible genetic under-pinnings of trans experience (e.g., Hare et al., 2009; Henningsson et al., 2005; Reiner & Gearhart, 2004). Neurologists and anatomists point science toward the possible brain anatomy differences and similarities that could provide an explanation for trans experience (e.g., Kruijver et al., 2000; Rametti et al., 2011a, 2011b; Zhou et al., 1995). Other biologists suggest maternal hormonal influences (e.g., Cohen-Kettenis et al., 1999; Green & Young, 2009). Purely psychological theories are not yet well equipped to participate in hypothesis generation about the origins of trans experience. This is because trans people exist even while classical conditioning and other theories of learning and reinforcement would predict the exact opposite. Take for example, a trans woman. If that trans woman was treated by everyone in her immediate social experience as a boy when she was younger, how is it that she was able to "resist" (or be immune to) all of the male socialization? Current psychological theories would predict that socialization creates identity based on principles of learning and behavior. Trans persons show that this explanation is obviously incomplete. Purely psychological theories would need to account for how some people – namely trans people – are able to "resist" gender socialization, while other people – and the vast majority as cis people – are not able to resist the same socialization pressures.

However, there is at least one intriguing new theory about how psychological processes might connect with biological presets or tendencies. Fausto-Sterling (2019) has recently argued that socialization before the age of three – an apparently neglected research area in behavioral science for studying identity dynamics – could interact with gene activations and postnatal physiological processes to that point to create cis and trans experience. This idea is basically a model of embodied cognition for gender and the sense of self, and is purely theoretical at this time with no empirical studies to directly support it. Nonetheless, it is worth mentioning because it is one attempt to connect classic psychological theorizing with biological predispositions during infancy. Fausto-Sterling's basic premise is that from birth until the age of three years old, children are engaging with the world using all their sensory capacities (e.g., vision, touch, hearing) and that the sensations experienced – from caregivers and others interacting with the child – form the template for the child's sense of gender self-categorization. This is the meaning of "embodied cognition" – that, our sense experience forms the basis for and constrains our thoughts, feelings, and behaviors. Quite literally, Fausto-Sterling's argument is that how the child is treated from birth to three years old forms the child's self-concept of whether they are a boy or a girl or nonbinary. What is more, the origin of this self-concept is not easily remembered by almost anyone because most people do not have clear memories of these years (birth to three). Again, an intriguing argument but one without any studies to support it yet.

In sum, until all of the sciences get a sharper focus on basic research issues related to transgender populations, we will continue to have a difficult time answering what might appear to other scientists (or nonscientist observers) to be basic or preliminary questions.

3.1 Social and Legal Transitioning

Social Transitioning. At least one of us has argued that all transitions for transgender people are *social* in nature, while only some are legal and/or bodily (Tate et al., 2014). The social transition refers to the individual's behavior of changing some or many of their social presentations of gender to the larger world. Consider a trans woman, for example, who changes her pronouns to "she/her"; asks others to use those pronouns for her; grows her hair long; and starts to wear make-up and dresses in clothing and accouterments associated with the social group "women" in her culture. Any one of the listed behaviors would count as a social transition – different pronoun use, different accouterments, different clothing use. And, using that example as a case in the larger point, hopefully it is clear to the reader that social transitions take a variety of forms, but at base they concern changing how the self is viewed in social settings. Take another example, a trans man. He may change his pronouns to "he/him"; ask others to use those pronouns for him; yet, he may not change his hairstyle that much; he may already wear men's clothes and accouterments and continue to do so. He too has engaged in a social transition. Finally, consider a nonbinary person who only switches their pronouns to "they/them" and asks others to use those pronouns. This person may dress and behave in exactly the same manner as before, but they are now trans.

Legal Transitioning. Most industrialized countries, like the United States and the United Kingdom, attach a legal gender designation to a person's social experiences. Gender designations show up on government-issued identification (e.g., state ID cards, driver's licenses). Unsurprisingly, the gender designation usually refers to the person's birth-assigned category as either female or male – F or M. But, given the success of trans activism in the legal arenas of many national cultures, this gender can be changed to match the individual's self-assigned category rather than the birth-assigned category. In parts of the United States (e.g., California, Massachusetts), there is even a nonbinary designation that is neither F nor M, but another category (e.g., X). As one might expect, however, changing one's legal gender designator not only depends on the availability of that option in one's state, province, or country of residence, but it also almost always depends on paying fees. Advertising one's name change in a local newspaper and visiting a physician come with costs, as do the legal steps. Consequently, some transgender people in industrialized countries simply cannot afford to legally change their gender marker.

3.2 Bodily Transitioning

Bodies are a focus for many of the lived experiences of many people on the transgender spectrum. Many, but not all transgender people find it useful to make changes to their bodies or desire to do so (see Factor & Rothblum, 2008). It seems useful at present to consider that all choices about bodily changes are valid expressions of an individual's sense of self. Thus, bodily transition should be viewed as simply one way to define the concept of "transition" for transgender folks – one that often co-occurs with, but is secondary to, social transitioning.

Like the legal gender-marker change, bodily changes require some access to money and the larger healthcare system within any country. In the United States, some insurance companies pay for certain bodily surgeries or hormone supplements for transgender persons, sometimes with an age stipulation (e.g., before twenty-five years old). Of course, other insurance companies do not offer payments because they consider surgeries and hormones as elective or cosmetic medical procedures. Given the sheer expense of bodily transition, it is currently only accessible to some segments of the population in countries like the United States that lack a universal healthcare. And, to that point, there has been a long-standing practice of transgender people throwing fundraising parties – or, in the modern Internet age, creating fundraising social media campaigns – to cover some or all of the medical expenses.

3.2.1 Hormone Therapy

For those who wish to change their bodies and can afford it, there are a variety of options. From the limited behavioral research that we have, it seems that a large number of transgender people take some type of hormone (e.g., Factor & Rothblum, 2008), variously referred to as *hormone replacement therapy* (HRT) or as *gender-affirming hormone therapy*. Several medical textbooks now cover the basics of hormone therapy, and there are also online resources, such as the one provided by the Transgender Center for Excellence (which is associated with the University of California, San Francisco Medical School): http://transhealth.ucsf.edu/protocols. To review the basis of hormone therapy here: as we noted, everyone produces estrogens and androgens in their bodies. The goal of hormone therapy is to either up-regulate or down-regulate existing hormone levels to make individuals more similar in these estrogen and testosterone levels to either cis women (usually trans women) or to cis men (usually trans men). For trans women, hormone therapy has two parts. In one part, trans women are given estrogen to increase their production of this hormone to bring about the bodily changes associated with high levels of estrogen, such as those found in cis women – larger breast size and more adipose on the hips, stomach, and arms. However, estrogen is not a testosterone agonist, meaning increasing levels of estrogen do not necessarily decrease testosterone production (Hembree et al., 2009). Thus, in the second part, trans women are usually given testosterone-blockers to down-regulate the amount of testosterone that the body produces. Blocking testosterone enhances the bodily changes brought about by giving estrogen.

For trans men, hormone therapy tends to have one part because testosterone is an estrogen agonist, meaning that increasing the amount of androgen erases or cancels the effects of estrogen (Hembree et al., 2009). Thus, trans men may be given testosterone to increase muscle mass throughout the body and increase hair growth across the body, including facial hair.

For nonbinary trans folks, there is not yet good documentation regarding hormone use. Factor and Rothblum (2008) have shown that use of hormone therapy is generally lower among nonbinary folks as compared to trans women and men. Why? One reason might be that there are so many different ways to be nonbinary. Another reason might be that nonbinary folks might use testosterone for a shorter time than trans men or use estrogen for a shorter time than trans women to create only what might be seen by medical professionals as "partial effects." In any case, there are important opportunities for the medical establishment by focusing on how, how much, and for what reasons nonbinary folks use hormones.

Puberty-slowing drugs. One aspect of hormone therapy may seem a bit esoteric, unless of course it concerns a body that is of interest to you, including that of your child or yourself: the use of drugs to slow down the onset of puberty. Imagine yourself to be the parent of an eleven-year-old male who feels certain he wishes to live as a girl. You make predictions about the stability of the child's wishes and also cast your mind into an imagined future of your grown trans woman daughter. How will that future woman cope with a potential laryngeal prominence (colloquially called "a prominent Adam's apple"), a potentially deep voice, and potentially tall stature? You consult the pediatrician. Modern medicine understands the physiological changes that occur during puberty quite well – so much so that medical professionals can actually slow the pubertal process via physiological intervention. The process is often described in medical terms as using chemical agonists that block gonadotropin-releasing hormones (the latter initialized as GnRH; Lambrese, 2010). These GnRH agonists block the release of two main hormones in the pituitary gland, thereby preventing the release of estrogen and testosterone. Delivered early enough in human biological development, these GnRH agonists can effectively slow the progression of the tell-tale signs of puberty in the primary and secondary sex characteristics (e.g., further development of the genitals; breast budding; facial and genital hair growth). This slowing of the body's own pubertal process buys time before irreversible pubertal changes occur. This in turn allows transgender children in particular to receive affirming hormonal treatments (which were, in the past, described as cross-sex hormone treatments) in place of their own bodies producing unwanted or undesirable physical changes (e.g., Giordana, 2008; Lambrese, 2010).

A natural question for bioethics is whether pubertal suppression should be provided to transgender children. If so, should it be provided only to those who have already sought psychiatric intervention and been diagnosed with gender identity disorder or dysphoria? What about those who resist the label of dysphoria? Bioethicists note that there are good arguments for allowing pubertal suppression and good arguments against it (Giordana, 2008, Lambrese, 2010). As Giordana (2008) notes, the intervention appears to help reduce the high rate of suicide among adolescent and young adult trans people, allowing transgender children to grow into their evolving bodies like "normal" teenagers. On the other hand, some clinicians believe that puberty may be key to having children understand their true gender identity and that suppressing puberty does not allow this process to unfold (Lambrese, 2010).

3.2.2 Surgeries

Although manifold physical changes can be wrought by hormone therapies, two areas of the body remain virtually unchanged in appearance: the chest area and the genitals (internal and external). Some, but not all, trans people opt for some form of surgery to effect changes. Surgeries are not free, in a financial sense or any other; but some trans individuals feel the results are worth the costs.

Surgery on the chest area is less challenging than surgery on the genital area, perhaps in part because many cis individuals have needed chest surgery for decades. Consider first trans women. Although the addition of estrogen and the blocking of androgens make the breasts somewhat larger than their previous form, some trans women want to have larger and more prominent breasts. These trans women often seek a type of top surgery that is already called *breast augmentation* in the medical community. Plastic surgeons have been performing breast augmentation on cis women for decades and have advanced their techniques and materials. Older techniques of breast augmentation required large incisions on the underside of the breast to insert an implant to augment breast size. Newer techniques can create smaller incisions, including through the areola, in a type of "reverse keyhole procedure," to insert the implant with minimal scarring.

For trans men, testosterone does make the chest area more muscular, but the fatty tissue inside the breasts and the mammary glands do not usually become smaller. Thus some trans men wish to have top surgery, which in this case means removal of the fatty breast tissue and reduction or removal of the mammary glands. Additionally, some trans men are concerned about the size of the areola and nipple, and this type of top surgery can also reduce the size of these structures. Top surgeries for trans men fall under the medical heading of *mastectomies* (literally "removing the mammaries"). Because medical professionals have performed mastectomies for decades as one way to manage or eliminate breast cancer, this type of top surgery for trans men is fairly routine nowadays. It seems that two different surgical approaches are currently favored. The traditional form of top surgery can create deep scarring on the underside of the pectoral muscles. In the newer "keyhole procedure," fatty tissue is removed through small incisions, usually in or near the areola. The older technique may still be preferred by individuals who had worn a bra with larger than a (US) B-size cup while the newer procedure may be favored by individuals who had smaller breasts.

What about the genitals? Many in the trans community feel worried about the obsession of cis people, even allies, with their external genital structures. Our belief is that information demystifies processes and that demystification can help everyone.

Differentiating between internal and external genitalia, there may be good reasons for trans women to have their testes removed. If the gonads are removed before puberty, androgen production will be greatly diminished and thus the individual may not undergo some of the secondary changes – such as the lowering of voice – that occur during adolescence. Whenever done, removal of the testicles means that the individual is free from the later risk of testicular cancer.

For surgery on the external genitalia, several options existed for trans women in the past; but today the most consistently used is the modern vaginoplasty (literally "vagina construction"), whose name masks the fact that a vulva is created as well. In this type of bottom surgery, the penis is surgically inverted (and literally turned inside out), then inserted into the space between the prostate and the anus. The head of the penile structure (called the glans) is left intact with its nerve endings attached to form the person's clitoris. (As we noted above, the glans of the penis is the same structure as the clitoris.) The former penile shaft (now inverted) becomes the new vaginal canal. The urethral tube remains encased by the glans, so, unlike cis women, trans women with surgery urinate through their clitoris (while cis women have a separate urethral opening underneath the clitoris). Because of the homo-materiality of the penile shaft and the vaginal canal, the new vagina self-lubricates with sexual excitement. Finally, the scrotal skin is flattened to form the new labia major (outer lips).

In trans men, a full hysterectomy will eliminate menstruation and make it impossible for a pregnancy to occur. Removal of the ovaries, fallopian tubes, and uterus also removes the risk of ovarian, uterine, or cervical cancer. For trans men's external genitals, testosterone enlarges the clitoris; yet some trans men may wish to have a surgically constructed penis and scrotum. For trans men's bottom surgeries, several options have existed in the past, but a recent option is to engage in what is called a *phalloplasty and scrotoplasty* (literally "phallus construction" and "scrotum construction") that uses the man's genital tissue and skin from either his forearm and from his inner thigh. In this type of surgery, the skin of the forearm or thigh creates the outer skin of the penile shaft and is connected with nerves and blood vessels of the existing genital issue. When an erectile device is also surgically implanted, phalloplasty may allow for erections. The existing urethral duct is connected to a new urethral duct to extend it through the length of the new penile shaft, permitting urination via the new penis. While some people choose to leave the labia majora opening intact others

Male to Female Vaginoplasty

The penile-scrotal skin tube is turned inside-out and inserted into the space between the bladder and prostate, and the rectum

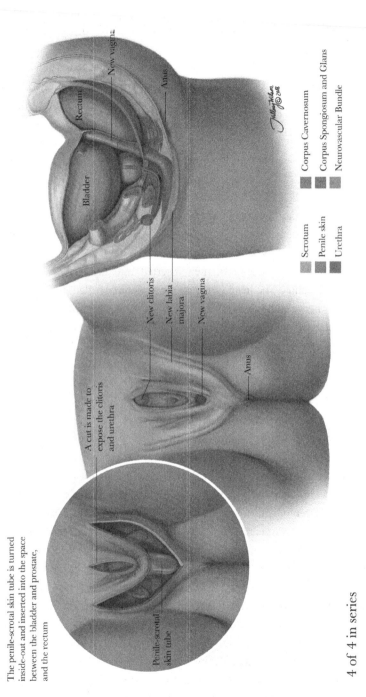

Penile-scrotal skin tube

A cut is made to expose the clitoris and urethra

New clitoris

New labia majora

New vagina

Anus

Bladder

Rectum

New vagina

Anus

Scrotum

Penile skin

Urethra

Corpus Cavernosum

Corpus Spongiosum and Glans

Neurovascular Bundle

Figure 3 Male to female vaginoplasty

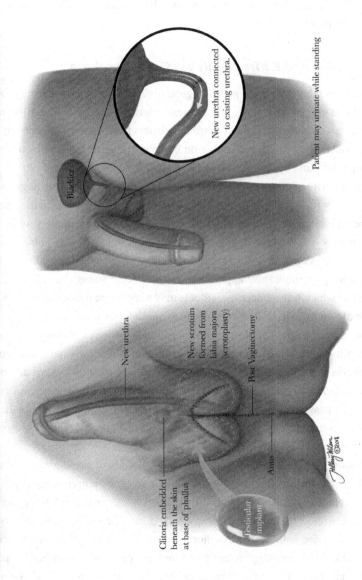

Forearm Flap Phalloplasty Stage 2: Urethral lengthening and scrotoplasty

Bladder

New urethra connected to existing urethra.

Patient may urinate while standing

New urethra

New scrotum formed from labia majora (scrotoplasty)

Post Vaginectomy

Clitoris embedded beneath the skin at base of phallus

Testicular Implant

Anus

Figure 4 Forearm flap phalloplasty

choose to have their labia majora (outer lips) sewn together to create the scrotal structure. The new scrotal sac can be filled with cosmetic testicles – the same kind developed for cis men who lose one or both testicles to testicular cancer. The skin of the forearm or the inner thigh is quite sensitive to the touch, and thus trans men can (re)learn to become aroused by stimulation of this skin now on their new penis.

3.2.3 Treatments and Gender Dysphoria

Individuals who experience psychological distress because of the incongruence between their gender identity and the gender assigned at birth are said to suffer from *gender dysphoria*. Gender dysphoria differs from gender nonconformity in that gender nonconformity focuses on behavior rather than feelings or cognitions (American Psychiatric Association, 2016).

The severity of gender dysphoria varies. Some children, as early as two years of age, may feel anger for being born as the wrong gender or "the wrong body." Some transgender adults report increased feelings of stress, anxiety, or depression as they live their lives conforming to their assigned gender at birth. Other transgender people may not feel high levels of stress and discomfort, even if they wish to change their appearance or their legal status (Lev, 2013a). The extent to which transgender individuals may experience gender dysphoria may associate with social and cultural factors (Shirdel-Havar et al., 2019).

Some transgender people seek hormonal and/or surgical therapy as a means for dealing with gender dysphoria. Seen from another angle, an expression of dysphoria is one means to help assure that insurance pays for at least part of the cost of hormonal and surgical therapy. Indeed, according to the Standards of Care for transgender people one of the criteria for prescribing hormonal therapy and/or genital surgery is persistent and well-documented gender dysphoria (Coleman et al., 2012).

Among people who seek and go through hormonal or surgical treatment, level of satisfaction is generally high and a sense of regret is generally low (Byne et al., 2012; Coleman et al., 2012; Green & Fleming, 1990; Wiepjes et al., 2018). Consistently, hormone therapy and surgical procedures alleviate symptoms associated with gender dysphoria. Follow-up studies of hormonal and/ or surgical intervention suggest that those increase patients' self-esteem, capacity for sexual satisfaction, body image, and happiness (Byne et al., 2012; Green & Fleming, 1990; van de Grift et al., 2017). The success of the hormonal and or surgical treatment depends on a number of factors. The younger the patient, the greater the satisfaction. Family support is also critically important in increasing levels of happiness.

4 Multifaceted Model of Gender

Just as biological sex is a summary term that includes various components, so does the term gender. As we have said earlier, any serious investigation of the transgender experience opens our eyes to the fluidity of gender and to the complexity of the very concept of gender. We find ourselves discarding the old simplistic views about gender as soon as we question the gender binary.

Gender includes a number of dimensions or facets. A useful way to conceptualize the many meanings of gender is to take the perspective that gender is a bundle of different phenomena. Figure 5 presents the *facet model of gender* (Hyde et al., 2019; Tate et al., 2014). The usefulness of the facet model is that it collects the meanings of gender that scholars want to think about across the social and behavioral sciences. Although all the facets relate to each other, we can analyze them separately.

4.1 Assigned Gender at Birth

The first facet, birth-assigned gender category, corresponds roughly, but imperfectly, to biological sex. As we have noted, in industrialized societies, cultural authorities such as obstetricians, pediatricians, and other adults assign a gender to the newborn. Almost always they do so on the basis of visual inspection of the external genitalia. Hardly ever does the assignment to one sex or the other depend on components of biological sex (chromosomes, internal genitalia, hormonal levels) other than the external genitalia.

Gender assignment at birth is utility in medical science because it allows for the imperfect but generally accurate prediction of pubertal and postpubertal hormone levels of both androgens and estrogens. Yet, it is important to

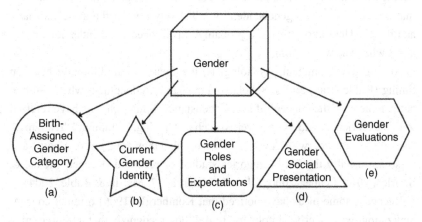

Figure 5 Gender as a bundle of phenomena

remember that the naming of genital forms using gender terms helps set into motion a host of other phenomena that are interpersonal. Using their own preconceptions, parents or legal guardians of newborns make assumptions about what the baby's likes, interests, and preferences will be or should be. Assumptions help shape the behaviors of parents and other caregivers which, in turn, have consequences for how the baby experiences the world through the earliest developmental stages of infancy, toddlerhood, and then adolescence – and likely beyond those stages.

In the present time, social media can amplify problems. Parents are encouraged to "reveal" uniquely and creatively the gender of their child in parties (e.g., exploding cakes with pink or blue fillings), creative social media posts using games (e.g., Scrabble), and merchandise (Gieseler, 2018). With gender being determined and announced even before birth, the assigned sex facet of Figure 5 can be viewed as others' categorization of the individual, and further sets into motion how that individual person is socially perceived, controlled, and encouraged or discouraged to behave (Hyde et al., 2019).

4.2 Current Identity

Meanwhile, there are other phenomena at play, collected under the heading of the *current identity* facet in Figure 5. Current identity refers to the well-known, and somewhat adequately studied experiences of children coming to understand their location in the world in terms of a gender category. Originally Lawrence Kohlberg (1966) proposed that children come to an understanding during their early years that they are a girl or a boy and that they will remain a girl or boy. The term gender constancy refers to the concept, which generally solidifies at some point in preschool development, that a person's own self-label and other people's self-labels will remain the same over time. Children know, for instance, that an adult woman's gender identity will likely remain the same into later adulthood. They know that she probably experienced her gender identity as a girl when she was a child.

Among developmental psychologists, the focus has traditionally been on timing (Ruble et al., 2007). Scholars have sought to document when children come to acquire the concept of gender constancy. Some scholars have referred to this experience with various verbs, such as "having," "finding," "realizing," "accepting," or otherwise developing a sense that they are a girl or a boy – and these are usually the only categories studied or recorded (Keener, Mehta, & Smirles, 2017; Leaper, 2000; Liben & Bigler, 2017; Martin & Ruble, 2004)

Recently, some of us have noticed that Kohlberg's (1966) original conceptualization was overly simplistic. It did not recognize that children may distinguish between their private understandings and outward or public presentation (Tate, 2014; Tate, et al., 2014). As an example case, a trans boy may (a) *privately* self-categorize as "boy" and (b) *privately* pay attention to the gender norms for boys but (c) may *publicly* allow references to himself and then later self-reference (based on social pressures) as "girl." The trans child may, thus, have a much more complicated and sophisticated analysis of self than Kohlberg imagined. Of course, the same split between privately held views and views that are shared also applies to cis children, especially as the children come to understand that it is not safe to share some of their private thoughts with caregivers.

Some psychology researchers have begun to focus on current identity dynamics during childhood and early adolescence in a manner consistent with the implications from Tate et al.'s (2014) gender bundle understanding and Aaron Devor's (2004) conceptual model of transgender development. Kristina Olson and her colleagues, for example, have examined self-concepts using standard cognitive psychology tasks to show that trans girls and trans boys appear to have self-concept representations – as either girl or boy, respectively – that are (statistically) indistinguishable from cis girls and cis boys, respectively, who are of the same age and other similar demographic characteristics (e.g., Olson, Key, & Eaton, 2015; Olson & Gülgöz, 2017). Additionally, when supported by their families, trans girls and boys have mental health outcomes that are basically the same as cis girls and boys who are matched on relevant demographic characteristics (e.g., Olson et al., 2016; Olson & Gülgöz, 2017). Taken together, the empirical findings support the implications and predictions from transgender theorists (viz., Devor; Tate) that current identity dynamics appear to be symmetrical between trans and cis experiences of gender self-categorization.

4.3 Gender Roles

As children develop, other experiences become very salient to them – namely interpersonal experiences and the expectations of social interactions that coincide with or are based on gender. In Figure 5, we refer to these experiences as the *gender roles, expectations, and ideologies* facet. Gender roles and ideologies are probably the most socially well-known of the facets of the gender bundle. Gender roles are the known expectations for how people in different gender groups are supposed to behave in a society.

Some cultures view gender roles as complementary – meaning that one gender group is expected to have the qualities that another gender group lacks, and vice versa – while other cultures view gender roles as more equal or similar. In any event, much time in childhood is spent figuring out how one is expected by caregivers and peers to behave based on being a girl or a boy (Bem, 1983; Helgeson, 2016; Thorne, 1993). This mental work continues as children enter adolescence and then adulthood.

Of course, individuals are not passive vessels only taking in and being completely guided by other's expectations. Instead, individuals consider how comfortable they feel when they behave consistently or inconsistently with the gender roles of their time and place. In general, people may feel comfortable with some gender role expectations for their gender group but not with others; comfortable with all the gender role expectations for their gender group; or comfortable with none of the role expectations for their gender group.

Considerations about gender roles are also complicated by factors such as sexual orientation. In the United States, for example, heterosexuality may feed into complementary gender role expectations for women and men. For example, those who subscribe to a heterosexual norm might assume that women should be emotionally available and emotionally supportive of men but not agentic, on one side; and that men should be more competitive, stoic (or less emotional), and be financial providers for women, on the other side (Glick & Fiske, 1997). Thus, even if a woman is uncomfortable with some gender role expectations, if she is heterosexual, she may find that her partner pool of heterosexual men pulls her in the direction of society's gender role expectations.

4.4 Gender Presentation (or Performance)

Yet another set of experiences that are referred to as "gender" is the *social presentation of gender* – the fourth of the five facets depicted in Figure 5. This set of experiences is often lumped together with gender roles but deserves to be separated. One of the easiest ways to think about what we mean by social presentation is to think about phrases like "gender performativity" and all the behavioral manifestations that one can think of that correspond to that phrase (Martin, 1998; West & Zimmerman, 1987).

The behaviors that people engage in to express their gender identity or that are associated with gender are numerous. In industrialized societies, apparel and accoutrements (e.g., jewelry, makeup) constitute one way to "perform" gender. Entire industries are devoted to curating and selling women's apparel and men's apparel. One of the obvious uses of these apparel styles in society is to determine whether a stranger is a woman or a man. Presumptively, individuals buy and wear apparel in part at least to convey messages to others about their gender self-labeling.

Another way to perform gender is to modulate one's vocal pitch. In many industrialized societies, women are expected to speak with a higher pitch to their voices and men are expected to speak with a lower pitch. While everyone knows that there is variability in voice pitch within and between gender categories, the expectation allows strangers to infer another person's gender category. Transgender people often change their voice pitch to fit social conventions for their category (Lev, 2013a). The mis-gendering of intersex people because of gender-nonconforming voice pitch can be distressing (Nygren et al., 2019).

Names communicate gender. The names "Charlotte," "Ella," and "Faye" would lead most English speakers to believe that these individuals are women. Similarly, the names "Carl," "Elmer," and "Frank" would lead most English speakers to believe that these individuals are men. "Chris" presents ambiguities.

How people move their bodies is yet another way to perform gender (Henley, 1977; 1995; Pascoe, 2011). In the United States, women are taught from a young age to walk by rolling their hips more than their shoulders, while men are taught to engage in the opposite pattern. Likewise, women are taught to cross their legs when seated, while men are taught to (or allowed to) keep their legs open when seated.

Gender performativity shifts according to context (Deaux & Major, 1987; Mehta, 2015). When young girls play with other girls, they tend to be more agentic compared to when they play with boys when they often turn more passive (Maccoby, 1990). When adolescent boys and girls play with each other, boys tend to increase their level of femininity while girls' level of femininity remains the same (Leszczynski & Strough, 2008). In a study done with college students, men reported greater levels of masculinity when they were with other men compared to when they were with female students; the opposite result was found for women who tended to report a greater sense of femininity with other women compared to when they were with men (Mehta & Dementieva, 2017). These results show that being in certain contexts shifts how people perform and understand their gender and the extent to which they identify as masculine or feminine.

4.4.1 Gender Performance, Sexuality, and Sexual Orientation

The context of heterosexual relationships in the United States requires women to exaggerate stereotypically feminine traits and men to exaggerate stereotypically masculine traits. Indeed, heterosexuality reinforces its status as being "natural" by framing people with penises as naturally more masculine, aggressive, and agentic, and as the subject of sexual desire, while those with vaginas are framed as naturally more feminine, nurturing, and passive, and as the object of sexual desire (Glick & Fiske, 1997). Cultural practices and values link masculinity to male bodies (e.g., masculine bodies are strong bodies) and femininity to female bodies (e.g., women's breast are nurturing life). Naturalizing masculinity and femininity into male and female bodies makes heterosexuality, which brings together these two "complementary" traits, appear normal, universal, and natural (Balzer Carr, Ben Hagai, & Zurbriggen, 2017; Bem, 1995; Butler, 1990). Such heterosexual scripts accentuate cisgender performances; think of the teenage girl spending hours applying lipstick and nail polish and prancing around in very short and very pink shorts. Think of the teenage boy using his free time in front of the mirror flexing his muscles, practicing how to deepen his voice, and dreaming of a date.

Since traditional gender performance is linked to heterosexuality, those who deviate from conventional gender performances are suspected of homosexuality. Historically, transgender people were categorized as a type of homosexual. People who were assigned male at birth but expressed their gender in a feminine manner were seen by others as doing so because of their desire to sleep with men; people assigned female at birth who performed their gender in a masculine manner were seen as wishing to have sex with women (Meyerowitz, 2009). Such historical misconceptions and prejudices that link transgender identity to homosexuality are still prevalent in certain misinformed and/or transphobic discourses.

Sexual orientation is a modern scientific phrase that describes the observation that people tend to orient toward certain groups of other people (usually based on gender labels) for sexual and emotional attraction (Savin-Williams, 2009). Scientists also agree that, for humans, sexual orientation is multidimensional. Sometimes this dimensionality is referred to as the ABCs of sexual orientation. The "A" stands for "attraction," and refers to a desire for sexual contact with certain people. An emotional attraction may also be part of the "A," although for some people sexual and emotional attractions are focused on different kinds of people. The "B" stands for "behavior," and refers to the types of people with whom a person actually has sex or wants to have sex (especially if a person has not had sex yet). The "C" stands for "categorization," and refers to the label (or category) that a person would use to describe his- or herself to others – usually in order to succinctly express the "A" and "B" dimensions (Savin-Williams & Diamond, 2000).

The proliferation of gender categories is also associated with a trend toward the proliferation of sexual categories (Bem, 1995; Butler, 1990; Halberstam, 2017). Individuals who are attracted to people regardless of their gender may choose to identify as pansexual or polysexual (terms that move beyond binary assumptions of bisexual identity). Other people who prefer to be in multiple loving relationships may identify as polyamorous, and people who do not feel sexual attraction to others may choose to identify as asexual (Cerankowski & Milks, 2010; Samons, 2009). Transgender people may identify with any of these sexual categories or may choose to identify with more traditional categories such straight, gay, lesbian, or bisexual. Finally, some people may prefer not to categorize themselves in terms of attraction to a general gender category or gender identity.

A recent online survey of 506 trans people recruited from college campuses across the United States (through announcements at campus resource centers and LGBTQ groups) found that among undergraduate and graduate transgender students, only 3.4 percent identified as "heterosexual"(Goldberg et al., 2019). Another study of 292 transgender and gender-variant people recruited from different transgender and gender-variant groups (i.e., convenience sampling) found that 14 percent of the sample identified as heterosexual. Pansexual and queer were the most commonly endorsed sexual orientation (Kuper, Nussbaum, & Mustanski, 2012). Altogether, transgender may identify with a wide range of sexual identities including queer, pansexual, bisexual, gay, asexual, or straight.

Given that the "LGBTQ" expression lumps together both sexual and gender identities, are we uncomfortable with current references to the "LGBT community" or the "LGBTQ community"? The answer is no for two reasons. First, like people who defy heterosexist norms, people on the trans spectrum cannot be complacent about issues of gender. Second, like those in the LBG(Q) community, those in the trans community have often been stigmatized or marginalized by mainstream society.

The Term "Queer". Even though it invites confusion of gender identity with sexual orientation, the term *queer*, used in the sense of nonconforming, currently has utility. Consider a lesbian cis woman – let's call her Lucia – who began dating a partner whom Lucia thought was another cis woman. If Lucia's partner discloses that he is actually a trans man, Lucia might no longer consider herself a lesbian, but she might self-identify as queer. One factor among the many that may influence Lucia's decision to change sexual orientation labels may be that she can retain a self-concept that she is mostly attracted to women and now possibly to trans men too. The traditional understanding of "lesbian" does not convey this additional attraction to trans men specifically, but "queer" may function to convey some larger sense of not being heterosexual – even if she might be viewed as such by observers because she is with a man. Likewise, consider a cis man – let's call him Fred – whose is married to a cis woman. If Fred's "wife" transitions into being a trans man, the word "queer" might come in handy. Fred may not think of himself as gay, but he might identify as queer as a way to suggest that his attraction is mostly to cis women with additional attraction to one (trans) man. In this way, "queer" can be a very useful term for those with a view of the world that is not easily conveyed by labels that are too rigid to capture nuances within sexual attraction.

There is another reason to embrace the term queer. From a queer perspective, gender and sexuality are historical constructions grounded in power relations (Balzer-Carr, Ben Hagai, & Zurbriggen, 2017; Butler, 1990; Cohen, 1997; Foucault, 1978). Patriarchal power relations that enforced the submission of women to men throughout history also worked to construct a binary under-standing of gender. Queers reject this binary.

4.5 Gender Evaluations

The reality of stigma brings us to the last element depicted in Figure 5: *gender evaluations*. Individuals may see themselves as similar to or different from other people in their gender category (Egan & Perry, 2001). They may also favor those in the same gender category or those in another gender category, which is usually referred to as "sexism" (Spence, 1993). Thus, for example, a woman may see herself as typical of all women, and yet she may overvalue men and undervalue women.

It seems that most people in all cultures have sex stereotypes. These stereo-types are often produced and reinforced by unequal distribution of resources between people in society. In patriarchal societies, in which men hold most of the wealth and political leadership, sex stereotypes depict women as less capable and worthy compared to men. Anti-women stereotypes rationalize and justify women's lower social status and lack of accesses to resources (Baldner & Pierro, 2019; Glick & Fiske, 1997; Robnett, 2016).

The five-facet model of gender proves a useful tool when we wish, as observers, to understand the experience of being on the trans spectrum. By differentiating between various facets of identity, we see that a trans identity involves a conflict between two components: gender assigned at birth and gender identity. We note that gender roles, gender performance, and gender evaluations are distinct from the gender identity one feels for oneself and the gender identity assigned by experts.

4.6 Burgeoning Research on Transgender and Gender-Nonconforming Children

With the understanding that gender is multifaceted, we can now turn to some of the burgeoning or still developing research on transgender and, separately, gender-nonconforming children. The perspective that gender is multifaceted will help the reader understand this new research in a deeper way and a way that is consistent with the latest scientific theorizing about gender.

There are diverse trajectories for the emergence of transgender identity. Some people know they are transgender at a later stage of their lives and some know at a very young age (McGuire et al., 2016). A transgender child may assert to their parents a gender different than the parent's perception of them. For instance, one mother of a transgender child named Lilly thought she had a son, but her daughter told her when she was four years old that she "had a girl's heart, brain, and soul" (Kuvalanka et al., 2014, p. 359). In recent years, reports from different gender clinics indicate a large increase in the number of transgender children who are seeking help and services (Nealy, 2017; Spack et al., 2012). Recent research and treatment of transgender children is rooted in a gender-affirming paradigm (Ehrensaft, 2014; Lev, 2013a; Nealy, 2017). If in the 1980s and 1990s transgender children were seen as socially malleable and encouraged to learn behavior that confirmed to their gender assigned at birth, in the 2000s a new gender affirming paradigm has emerged that focuses on the diversity of gender expressions in human populations (Cohen-Kettenis & Pfäfflin, 2010; Coleman et al., 2012; McGuire et al., 2016; Olson, 2016; Olson, Key, & Eaton, 2015). This new paradigm of research and clinical treatment of transgender children aims to listen to children and affirm children's gender identity, even when this identity does not fall within the traditional understanding of every child as essentially cisgender. Moreover, this paradigm focuses on the ways in which gender dysphoria is not an inherent part of the transgender experience but rather is derived from society's oppressive treatment of transgender and non-binary children and adults (Coleman et al., 2012).

Transgender and gender nonconforming children. At two years of age, some children's gender identification doesn't match how others categorize them. These children assert a gender different than the gender they were assigned at birth. A feeling that they are categorized into the wrong gender by others may become clear to some children at the age of two, five, or later in their lives. Some children who do not conform to their assigned gender during childhood persist to physically transition when they are teenagers or adults (usually 2–27 percent of children visiting clinics in childhood); other children who are gender non-conforming may desist feeling alienated from their birth gender when they enter adolescent (Steensma et al., 2011). Differences between persisters and desisters are associated with the content of their discontent. Persisters (children who begin social and physical transition in adolescents) are more likely to feel that they are a different gender, which is in-line with the idea of the current gender identity facet in the multifaceted understanding of gender discussed by Tate et al., (2014). Desisters are more likely to express a feeling that they want to engage in *behaviors* traditionally associated with the other gender or wish to be part of the opposite gender group in terms of social expectations, which would be consistent with the idea of gender roles and expectations in the multifaceted understanding of gender (see Olson, 2016, Steensma et al., 2011).

Gender identity development. Psychological research on gender identity development suggests that as early as the age of two children can categorize themselves into a gender category. Children's identification with a particular gender category (e.g., being a boy or a girl) motivates them to seek peers who share their gender group (Martin, Ruble, & Szkrybalo, 2002). With the help of peers and adults, children learn gender stereotypes and how to do gender correctly. Around six years of age children's endorsement of gender stereotypes, such as girls have long hair and boys have short hair, peaks and then decline in adolescents. During this time children's gender stereotyping is rigid and they tend to dislike people who do not confirm to traditional gender norms (Bem, 1993; Leaper & Farkas, 2015; Ruble et al., 2007). Children's early understanding of gender, especially for others, is relatively superficial in that they believe that certain visual or behavioral characteristics can change a person's gender. They also see gender as unstable, meaning it can change across time. At about seven years of age children achieve an understanding of gender as consistent and stable (Olson & Gülgöz, 2018).

Comparative research on cognitive gender development among children who socially transitioned compared to children who use the same label as their birth gender category suggests that both sets of children go through similar developmental milestones. Specifically, Olson and colleagues compared transgender children to gender conforming (typical) siblings, and a control group of gender conforming (typical) children of the same age. Transgender children were similar to their siblings and to the control group in seeing themselves as like other children with the same gender identity (Olson & Gülgöz, 2018). In an implicit association test, transgender children, like their siblings and a control group, matched images of children who share their gender identity with positive images such as ice cream faster than negative images such as a snake (Olson, Key, & Eaton, 2015). Transgender children were similar to other children in favoring images of same gender children, toys, and clothing (Fast & Olson, 2018). In terms of gender stereotype rigidity, transgender children didn't differ from their siblings or a control group in categorizing certain activities as appropriate for a stereotypical gender; for instance, girls should do gymnastics or boys should play video games (Fast & Olson, 2018). A more recent study with a larger and older sample of transgender children, their cisgender siblings, as well as a cisgender control group, found that transgender children and their siblings subscribed to gender stereotypes to a lesser degree, saw violations of gender stereotypes as more acceptable, and were more open to friendship with gender nonconforming children compare to a control group (Olson & Enright, 2018). Finally, in terms of gender constancy when asked if a child would change their gender if they wore opposite gender clothes or played opposite gender games, transgender children were slightly more likely to express gender constancy compared to cisgender children, but this difference was not statistically significant (Fast & Olson, 2018).

While cognitive gender development may be similar among transgender children and cisgender children, emotional development is more complex for transgender children. Transgender children are reported to experience higher levels of depression, anxiety, and suicidal ideation (Olson et al., 2016). Family members of transgender children are also likely to experience anxiety and depression (McGuire et al., 2016). Anxiety and depression among US transgender children and their family members is likely associated with the rigid enforcement of the gender binary in US culture. Furthermore, some sources of distress among transgender family members is associated with family conflict over how a transgender child's identity should be affirmed. Such conflict can happen between parents (e.g., different approaches between mothers and fathers), nuclear family and extended family (e.g., aunts or grandmothers), and the transgender child's parents versus the school system. Mothers who come to affirm and support their transgender child report that their child became less anxious, happier, and friendly to their peers (Kuvalanka et al., 2014).

A survey study of 73 transgender children who socially transitioned indicates that transgender children who are affirmed by their family did not show higher levels of depression or anxiety compared to normative peers as was previously found in samples with less supportive families (Olson et al., 2016). Further survey research examining parents and transgender or nonbinary children, also indicates normal levels of depression and anxiety among children whose gender nonconformity was affirmed. This survey further indicates that positive peer relations among transgender children served as the strongest predictor for wellbeing (Kuvalanka et al., 2017).

The findings that transgender children who have parents that affirm and support their identity do not have elevated levels of anxiety and depression highlights the importance of affirming children's gender identity. Such affirmation includes carefully listening to children's gender expression in order to understand how they see their own gender, using their chosen names and pronouns, and on a social level connecting children to transgender adults who are thriving, and helping them gain the support of their friends and their peers (see Ehrensaft, 2017; Lev, 2013a; Nealy, 2017).

5 Lived Experiences of Public Figures

Irritated by two small-minded women who mistake their misanthropy for feminism, Oshima, one of the central characters in Murakami's novel *Kafka on the Shore* (2005), blurts out the truth that he is a trans man. In the hour that follows, Oshima reaches out to a fifteen-year-old runaway who calls himself Kafka and who is the narrator of the novel. Says Oshima: "I know I am a little different from everyone else, but I am still a human being. That's what I'd like you to realize. I'm just a regular person, not some monster. I feel the same things everyone else does, act the same way" (Murakami, 2006, pp. 181–182). Oshima goes on to reflect: "Sometimes, though, that small difference feels like an abyss" (p. 182).

Memoirs and other writings of public figures tend to agree with the sentiments of the fictional character Oshima. Life can feel difficult to people whose current gender identity does not align with the identity assigned at birth.

In this section, we recount highlights from published memoires of trans women, trans men, and nonbinary people. Some of the individuals are not well known today, but many have become household words. Most of what the public knows about the experiences of trans people comes from publicity about these people, made famous by their own revelations and by accounts in the media. These personal stories circulated in the public sphere help illuminate and clarify the complexity of the transgender experience. In the accounts of different transgender people who have been public about their identity certain themes emerge. Consistent with the theorizing of Devor (2004) and Tate (2014), we can see in many of the accounts a split, usually starting in childhood, between the private self-label and what is presented to the outside world. We can see a struggle to conform with the gender expectations of society. We see struggle followed by some degree of acceptance by self. We provide the narratives below because collections of statistics do not always convey to most audiences the nuances of a lived life.

5.1 Trans Women

One of the most famous figures embodying medical understanding of the transgender experience is Christine Jorgenson. Christine was born in the Bronx in 1926 and she was assigned male at birth. She was drafted into the military to serve in World War II. Upon her return, she learned of the option for a "sex change" operation in Europe. She traveled to Copenhagen and returned to the United States looking like a very beautiful woman. Her beauty sparked a media frenzy. Newspaper headlines like "Ex-GI Becomes a Blond Beauty" and "Christine Ill at Ease" (Meyerowitz, 2009), began a public conversation on the "transgender condition." Reflecting on the media frenzy surrounding her, Jorgensen (1967) wrote:

> I'd been courted, derided, admired, made the subject of off-color jokes, and clothed in the light of half-truths and controversy. Apparently, there would be no attitudes in between complete hostility and total approval. I was going to be like eggplant – one either liked it very much, or not at all. (Ames, 2005, p. 75)

The exposure that Jorgensen received was a watershed moment in transgender history in which the word *transsexual* was coined to distinguish people who sought surgical transformation from transgender-identified people (like some cross-dressers and transvestites) who did not (Stryker, 2008).

5.1.1 In the World of Sports

Two key figures contributed a great deal to transgender visibility during the 1970s: Jan Morris and Dr. Renée Richards. Jan Morris was a famous British travel writer who covered the first ascent of Mount Everest and wrote over twenty-five books. Especially famous is her memoir *Conundrum* that came out in 1974. In it she explains her desire to be seen as a woman:

> I was three or perhaps four years old when I realized that I had been born in the wrong body, and should really be a girl ... by every standard of logic, I was patently a boy ... I had a boy's body. I wore boy's clothes. It is true that my mother wanted a daughter, but I was never treated as one. (Morris, 2005/ 1974, p. 4)

Notice that Morris makes the distinction between how she was treated by other people based on her assigned sex category (as a son and not as a daughter) and implies that people treated her in terms of gender role expectations based on her assigned category even though, all the while, she had a private, internal sense of self that was decidedly "girl" as her self-assigned identity. What is more, Jan Morris's sense of self-categorization as a girl persisted throughout childhood and into adolescence and eventually adulthood. Interestingly, Morris tried to hide from others her self-assigned identity as girl then woman.

Another important transgender figure that emerged in the 1970s is Dr. Renée Richards.

Richards was assigned male at birth, but, as a child, Richards remembers sneaking into her sister's bedroom and wearing her sister's clothes. At Yale University, Richards was considered a "golden boy" – a star student who was the captain of the tennis team (Drath, 2011). After Yale, Richards went on to become a leading eye surgeon, and saved the eyesight of many infants, children, and adults. After marrying a model and having a child, Richards continued to compete in amateur tennis competitions. Richard's need to present as a woman increased over the years. Rumors circulated among her community of friends in New York about Richards being spotted in women's clothes. Richards could not contain the desire to present as a woman, and eventually left her family to pursue a "sex-change" operation.

Richards began living as a woman in California, where she was recruited to participate in a tennis tournament. As she advanced in the league, she was outed as a transgender woman. Her participation in women's tennis became a media frenzy. Tennis players refused to play her or walked off the court. Richard's story began an ongoing debate on the role of transgender athletes within a sport system segregated by binary genders (Richards & Ames, 1983).

The debate over transgender and intersex participation in sports continues today and has become more complex with increased transgender visibility. Transgender adolescents coming of age in today's society are struggling to find safe spaces to compete within binary sports. For example, Terry Miller and Andraya Goodyear are two transgender track and field athletes who competed for their high school. They both won state titles for their fast running. In turn, three Connecticut girls who compete in high school track filed a federal discrimination complaint stating the state policy that allows transgender athletes like Miller and Goodyear to compete based on their gender identity has created an uneven playing field that cost them college scholarships.

In the highest levels of competitive sports, debates over gender are also raging. Since 2004, the International Olympic Committee (IOC) allowed transgender athletes to compete at the Olympics but only if they had gender reassignment surgery. In 2016, the IOC changed the guidelines and allowed any transgender man (FtM) to compete in the men category, but only transgender women whose testosterone level was below 10 nmol/L (for at least two months prior to competition) were allowed to compete in the women category. In April 2018, the International Association of Athletics Federations (IAAF) announced new "differences of sex development" rules that required athletes with specific disorders of sex development, testosterone levels of 5 nmol/L and above, and certain androgen sensitivity to take medication to lower their testosterone levels. This rule put star runner Caster Semenya, an Olympic gold medalist from South Africa, in jeopardy. When Semenya's testosterone levels were found to be above 5 nmol/L limit, she was barred from competing in the World Championship.

People supporting transgender athletes have argued that testosterone is not consequential to performance. Indeed studies suggest that higher testosterone levels do not predict winning in most athletic sports (Harper, Martinez-Patino,

Pigozzi, & Pitsiladis, 2018). Some advocates for transgender inclusion in sports argue that athletes never start at a level playing field and that sports select for different kinds of bodies; for instance, some athletes come from richer countries and have more resources to train compared to those from poorer countries. Some athletes, like Michelle Phelps, are born with super long arms that give them their edge in their sport (Petrow, 2016). People who support regulation on transgender people point out that, on average, females have 2.5–3 nmol/L levels of testosterone and the current limit of 10 nmol/L or 5 nmol/L is significantly above that. Others argue that testosterone during body development gives men an advantage, including larger hearts and lungs as well as muscle memory that under training can produce more force (Worrall, 2019). The debate that Renee Richards sparked continues to this era, a time of greater inclusion and visibility for transgender people.

5.1.2 In the Entertainment World

Within the entertainment industry, more trans women have stepped into the public view, in recent years. Janet Mock has authored articles and books, produced films, appeared on many talk shows discussing her life as an inter-racial, transgender woman from a poor background, and recently produces and writes for the television series *Pose*, which centers on trans women of color in New York's queer ballroom culture in the 1980s and 1990s. Before making her transition public, Mock was a successful editor at *People Magazine*. In an interview with *Marie Claire*, Mock revealed that she was assigned the male gender at birth (Mock & Mayo, 2011). In her memoir, Mock described her gender identity: "I was certain I was a boy, just as I was certain of the winding texture of my hair and the deep bronze of my skin. It was the first thing I'd learned about myself as I grew aware that I existed" (Mock, 2014, p. 15). However, Mock's "certainty" about being a boy was not long-lasting. When Mock began to learn about the world, she developed a "desire to step across the chasm that separated me from the girls – the ones who put their sandals in the red cubbyholes" (Mock, 2014, p. 15). Thus, although she was taught through other people's treatment of her that she was a boy, and initially accepted this, as her sense of self developed Mock realized her own internal sense of gender was that of a girl. This part of Mock's narrative reveals that initial socialization may have a profound influence on what a child *initially believes*. However, as a child develops, their own self-concept becomes clearer and clearer to them. In the case of many trans kids, the self-concept is one that this not the same as what the social authorities expected and reinforced.

The dissonance between the sex a person is assigned to at birth and the subconscious understanding, inclination, or intuition of a different gender identity is common in the identity narratives of transgender people. Julia Serano (2007), an important transgender writer, situates this dissonance at the heart of the transgender experience. She writes, "mental tension and stress that occur in a person's mind when they find themselves holding two contradictory thoughts or views simultaneously – in this case, subconsciously seeing myself as female while consciously dealing with the fact that I was male [to the rest of the world]" (p. 85) is a large source of the internal distress of coming to term with oneself as transgender.

Socializing agents and social norms enforce cisgender presentation while trans allies and other trans mentors can shield against social pressures to conform. As a young child, Mock attempted to express her femininity by wearing dresses, and she was immediately punished by her family. Nevertheless, her experience growing up in Hawaiian culture that has a third-gender category of Māhū (represents both man and woman) allowed her an exposure to transgender women at a relatively young age. Her transgender best friend Wendy shared estrogen pills with Mock. The pills allowed Mock to start her transition process before she passed through puberty. By her junior year of high school, Mock socially transitioned, adopting the name Janet after her childhood hero Janet Jackson. Mock recognized "my presence as a fifteen year old transgender must have been radical to many but for me it was the truth, and my truth led me to form a womanhood all of my own" (Mock, 2014, p. 146).

Another figure who has played a role in increasing transgender visibility is Candis Cayne. Like Janet Mock, Cayne grew up in Hawaii; unlike Mock, she began her transition process later in life at the age of 24, while living in New York City (Cayne & Jones, 2017). According to her memoir (Cayne & Jones, 2017) she had a twin brother and grew up in a middle-class home. She remembers being asked throughout her childhood if she was a boy or a girl. Around the age of seven, she visited her cousins Tanya and Teller who were also twins. Wrote Cayne:

> I remember vividly the minute when I thought, I'm supposed to be like her (i.e., Tanya) . . . we were running through a field. I was having so much fun, and Tanya turned to me and I thought at that moment, what happened? Why wasn't I born like her? (Cayne & Jones, 2017, para. 2)

After winning a scholarship to a dance school, Candis moved to New York where she met many transgender women. She worked as a drag queen. Unlike many of her colleagues, Candis did not happily return to a male identity offstage. When her twin brother got married, he asked her to be his best man.

Candis went to the wedding as a man, but when she came home she was incredibly depressed. "Looking at myself in the mirror, feeling so sad, when suddenly I saw a lilac aura around myself – and it was then that I knew I needed to live my life as a woman." Cayne realized that she was "still the same person I was before; I just needed to change the physical to match my heart and my mind" (Cayne & Jones, 2017, para.2). Candis Cayne became the first transgender actor to play a recurring transgender character with her role in the primetime ABC drama *Dirty Sexy Money*. Her successful TV appearances and writing increased transgender visibility and inspired many transgender people.

One of the most important figures inspired by Candis Cayne was Laverne Cox. Cox describes Candis' *Dirty Sexy Money* role as a major influence on her own career. Cox gained fame through her part as a transgender inmate in the Netflix hit show *Orange Is the New Black*. Cox was the first trans person to be nominated for an Emmy in an acting category for her role.

Like Mock and Cayne, Laverne Cox also danced from an early age. Dance played a key role in saving her life. In childhood, Laverne was bullied because of her femininity. She attempted suicide at age eleven. Nevertheless, her talent for dance offered an escape and she was able to win scholarships for a private boarding school, then for Indiana University – Bloomington, and later for Marymount Manhattan College where she graduated with a Bachelor of Fine Arts. In New York, a group of transgender women she met gave her the courage to shift her identity from gender-nonconforming to transgender. She remembers:

> During my college years, I went from being gender nonconforming to being more and more femme. I would soon start my medical transition and living and identifying as female. As I started my transition, I knew I wanted to continue to perform and I often found myself performing in drag shows in the nightclub scene. (Cox, 2019, para, 6–7.)

Laverne Cox was the first trans person to appear on the cover of *Time Magazine* (Steinmetz, 2014) in an issue called "The Transgender Tipping Point." Her work as a transgender advocate has been openly political. In an interview with Katie Couric, she criticized the media's obsession with transgender surgical procedures, describing the interest as a way to objectify trans people. In this 2014 interview she argued:

> The preoccupation with transition and surgery objectifies trans people. And then we don't get to really deal with the real lived experiences. The reality of trans people's lives is that so often we are targets of violence. We experience discrimination disproportionately to the rest of the community . . . If we focus on transition, we don't actually get to talk about those things. (Lees, 2017, para. 3)

Another transgender woman who has used her spotlight to highlight the marginalization of transgender people is Lana Wachowski.

Lana is one of the Wachowski sisters, the famous transgender sisters who directed the *Matrix* movie trilogy. The Wachowski sisters were first known in popular media as the Wachowski brothers. Both sisters are very private about their personal life and transgender identity. They refused to be interviewed for many years. Nevertheless, in 2012, Lana Wachowski explained that the violence against transgender women like Gwen Araujo made her overcome her desire for anonymity. She summoned the courage to discuss her trans identity in order to dispel some of the fear and prejudice against transgender people. Discussing a memory of herself in third grade, Lana recalled:

> I remember the third grade. I remember recently moving and transferring from a public school to a Catholic school. In public school I played mostly with girls, I have long hair and everyone wears jeans and t-shirts. In Catholic school the girls wear skirts, the boys wear pants. I am told I have to cut my hair. I want to play Four Square with the girls but now I'm one of them – I'm one of the boys. Early on I am told to get in line after a morning bell, girls in one line, boys in another. I walk past the girls feeling this strange, powerful gravity of association. Yet some part of me knows I have to keep walking. As soon as I look towards the other line, though, I feel a feeling of differentiation that confuses me. I don't belong there, either. (Wachowski, 2012, Oct 24)

A couple of years after Lana Wachowski transitioned, her director sibling also came out as Lily. Bullied by tabloids, Lily released her own statement to the *Windy City Times*, a daily newspaper in Chicago:

> [T]hese words, "transgender" and "transitioned" are hard for me because they both have lost their complexity in their assimilation into the mainstream … I've been transitioning and will continue to transition all of my life, through the infinite that exists between male and female as it does in the infinite between the binary of zero and one. We need to elevate the dialogue beyond the simplicity of binary. Binary is a false idol. (Baim, 2016, March 8)
>
> The experience of the Wachowski sisters highlights the experience of some transgender people as defined by a type of crossing: while some cross to the other gender category, others see themselves transitioning and continue to transition in the infant space between the man and woman categories.

Similar to the Wachowski's, Caitlyn Jenner was known for many years in the popular media by her male persona – namely, as Bruce Jenner, a decathlete. In the Bruce Jenner persona, Caitlyn grew famous enough to appear on boxes of Wheaties cereal – a crowning achievement for male athletes across all sports at that time. Jenner became a household name when she joined the reality TV show *Keeping Up with the Kardashians* in 2007. In the show she was known as

Bruce Jenner, the husband of Kris Jenner, the father of Kendell and Kylie Jenner, and the stepfather of Kim, Kourtney, and Khloé Kardashian. In 2015, tabloids began to report gradual changes in Jenner's appearance. Rumors began circulating. The media frenzy around Jenner's identity was unprecedented, and on June 1, 2015, Jenner announced on Twitter that she is a woman. Jenner wrote, *"I'm so happy after such a long struggle to be living my true self. Welcome to the world Caitlyn. Can't wait for you to get to know her/me* (Jenner, 2015, June 1)." Soon after, she was photographed for a *Vanity Fair* cover by the photographer Annie Leibowitz and interviewed for an ABC special. In her memoir, Jenner described the relationship between her persona as Bruce and the welcoming of Caitlyn:

> Bruce won the Olympics. I lived as a man before I transitioned. I had a life as Bruce, and the more comfortable I became as Caitlyn, the more I actually embrace Bruce as a valuable part of my life. I obviously don't want to be called Bruce, but I am not going to bury him and send him to the "dead name" pile. There has to be some reality here, at least for me. You can't simply blot out your past, your beliefs, your interests. The life that you lived as a father and dad and husband, the accomplishments and failures, do not get sent to the trash with a click of the mouse . . . I remember crying when I received my new birth certificate from the state of New York stating that I am female and giving my name as Caitlyn Maria Jenner. They were tears of joy in seeing the correct gender marker on such an important legal document. But there were also tears of sadness that Bruce was gone, the birth certificate being official proof. (Jenner and Bissinger, 2017, para. 3–4)

In this quote, Jenner highlights the complex relationship some transgender people have with past assigned identities. Some transgender people put their old names and personae in the dead name pile and do not use those again, while others, like Jenner, see those as incomplete yet important parts of who they once were.

5.2 Trans Men

Unlike many trans women, some trans men were able to live as men without drawing much attention to themselves (Stryker, 2008). For instance, the jazz musician Billy Tipton was married to five women and raised three adopted sons. At his death, the paramedics asked his son, "Did your father ever have a sex change?" (Smith, 1998, June 2). Even in intimate settings, Billy was able to pass as a male jazz musician with the help of Ace bandages he wore around his breasts and a prosthetic penis. Tipton explained the bandages by telling close friends that he suffered a childhood accident in which his ribs were broken (Mills, 2017, September 9).

One of the first visible trans man pioneers, openly self-identified as transgender, was Reed Erikson. Erikson was educated as an engineer; in 1962 he inherited his family business worth 5 million dollars and turned it into a 40-million-dollar fortune. After his father's death, he contacted Harry Benjamin, the same doctor who was consulted by Christine Jorgeson and many other transgender people, and created a foundation to support Benjamin's work. This support allowed Benjamin to write his path-breaking book *The Transsexual Phenomenon*. Erikson also created the Erikson Educational Foundation (EEF) which produced pamphlets giving basic advice to transsexuals on how to change their names and find proper medical care (Stryker, 2008). Meanwhile, other physicians like the Danish doctors Erling Dahl-Iversen and Georg K. Stürup helped shift the understanding of transgender urges away from a psychoanalytic understanding to a medical understanding in which the impulse to live as a different gender than the assigned one is caused by hormonal and genetic processes (Meyerowitz, 2009).

Nourished by the work that Reed Erikson and like-minded medical professionals started, the activist Lou Sullivan dedicated himself to continuing it. Born in 1951 in Wisconsin, Sullivan documented his longing and fantasies to become a man. For instance, when he was eleven he wrote in his diary "*when we got home, we played boys.*" At the age of fourteen he wrote

> I want to look like what I am but don't know what someone like me looks like. I mean, when people look at me I want them to think – there's one of those people . . . that has their own interpretation of happiness. That's what I am. (Stryker, 2008, p. 144)

Sullivan's desire to be a boy was complicated by his love for his long-term boyfriend Tom (Rodemeyer, 2018). Sullivan was the first visible transgender man who identified as a gay man. His writing and advocacy were particularly important for contemporary distinctions between gender identity and sexual desire. In the 1980s, Sullivan contracted the HIV virus; in his activism and death, he helped inaugurate the transgender political movement of the 1990s (Stryker, 1999).

One of the most famous examples of a trans man in the public view is Chaz Bono. Chaz Bono's transition process was very public because he grew up in the public eye as the child of Cher and Sonny Bono. In one memorable TV episode of their show Sonny and Cher, Chaz's parents performed their hit song "I Got You, Babe" in front of millions of viewers with their beautiful child in their arms. In the Chastity Bono persona, Chaz was a frequent guest on *The Sonny and Cher Comedy Hour*. Cher tended to police Chastity's strong tomboy tendencies. In his memoir, Chaz remembers feeling he was a boy from an early age. The feminization of his body during puberty was especially hard for Chaz. At around the age of thirteen Chaz began to identify as a lesbian. Sexual encounters with women in which he took the masculine (top) position made him feel comfortable (Bono & Fitzpatrick, 2012).

As he matured, Chaz begin to realize that he didn't feel fully comfortable as a lesbian. Because of his own internalized transphobia and his sensitivity to the public nature of his family, he resisted the concept of changing his gender. In his memoir Bono wrote: "*I remember thinking of my desire to transition almost as a disease, wanting it to lie dormant, hoping it wouldn't come out of remission and wreak havoc in my life*" (Bono & Fitzpatrick, 2012, p. 161). Part of the reason that Chaz was adamant about keeping his desire to transition under wraps was because he was afraid of the public reaction as he and his family are public figures. At the age of forty, Chaz began transitioning. He hired a publicist to manage the media circus. He described feeling different once he had begun transitioning, including a much higher sex drive.

> But the single most significant change was how incredibly happy I felt. Every part of me felt liberated. I was starting to get comfortable in my body for the first time in my life. Confidence streamed through me. The more male I looked, the more male I felt, the more joyous I became. (Bono & Fitzpatrick, 2012, p.197)

Another important transgender man to increase trans men's visibility is Thomas Beatie, known as in public discourse as the "Pregnant Man." Thomas Beatie grew up in Hawaii. Part white and part Filipino, Thomas was invited to participate in beauty pageants as a teenager (Beatie, 2008). At twenty-four, Beatie transitioned into a man. In his memoir he wrote,

> for as long as I can remember, and certainly before I fully knew what this meant, I wanted to live my life as a man. When I was young, I was a tomboy: I dressed in boy's clothes, I did boy things, I resisted the trappings of girlhood – dolls, dresses, all of that. I identified with the male gender in every way. I never thought I was born in the wrong body, however, nor did I ever want to be anyone else. I was happy being me, because I knew who I was inside. (Beatie, 2008, p. 6)

Beatie took hormones and had chest surgery. Then Beatie and his wife decided to have a baby. Because his wife was infertile, Beatie stopped taking hormones; within six months he started menstruating again. When he became pregnant carrying the baby himself, tabloids and newspaper all over the world exploited the story with headlines like "He's Pregnant. You're Speechless" (Trebay, 2008, June 22). Beatie had two more healthy children after his first pregnancy.

Increasing transgender visibility are more figures such as the actor Brian Michael Smith who came out as transgender publicly when he played a transgender man on the hit TV show *Queen Sugar*. Before coming out as transgender, Smith played several male roles on TV shows like *Girls* and *Law and Order*. Also, important to increasing transgender visibility are Rocco Kayiatos, an American rapper and blogger, and the photographer Amos Mac who founded *Original Plumbing*, a quarterly magazine dedicated to trans male culture, in San Francisco in 2009. The publication offers images of trans men and tackles themes central to trans male culture.

5.3 Nonbinary

Not every trans person is a trans man or a trans woman. Some consider themselves nonbinary. Alok Vaid-Menon, for instance, is a gender-nonconforming performance artist and writer and uses the personal pronouns "they" and "them" – in the singular form. They wrote a successful poetry book called Femme in Public. Vaid-Menon explains their nonbinary identity. They argue:

> Being non-binary is not just about my gender, but also about rejecting dichotomies and oppositional thinking, affirming my own complexity and simultaneity.
> Being non-binary isn't just about being defined by my absence (I am not a man or a woman), but also by my abundance (I am far too expansive to be encapsulated by the gender binary). Being non-binary is about embracing my fluidity, my becoming, my journey without fixed destination. (Arora, 2018 June 20, parag 4)

While Vaid-Menon usually appears in artistic venues, Asia Kate Dillion is a non-binary actor who broke into mainstream television. Most notably Dillion plays Tylor Mason, a non-binary stock analyst working at hedge fund firm in the show *Billions*. Dillion's non-binary character led the MTV Awards to combine their gender-segregated categories.

Jiz Lee is another trailblazer for non-binary people's visibility. Lee was born in Hawaii, edited the book *Coming Out Like a Porn Star* (Lee, 2015), and produced films for Pink & White Productions that showcase diverse representations of queer sexuality. Lee also played the role of a dominatrix in the hit TV show *Transparent*.

Another example of a relatively visible non-binary person is Ivan Coyte. Coyte is a LGBTQI+ writer and performer. Coyte authored eleven books including *Tomboy Survival Guide* (2016), and *Gender Failure with Rae Spoon* (2014). In *Gender Failure*, Coyte explains that the emergence of the word "they" as a non-binary pronoun commonly used in the queer community allowed them to shift from a trans man identity to a non-binary one. They write:

> I started to meet a lot more people who went by the "they" pronoun. Most people in the queer community around me did not have any difficulty using it. In a space where non-binary pronouns had been largely accepted, I began to see the benefits of using them. It dragged me out for an identity that had been previously cemented because I thought being a man was the only way to move away from my assigned sex. In this community, I did not have to be male nor to be female. (Coyote & Spoon, 2014, "How I Got to 'They'" para. 6)

For Coyote, being seen as a trans man within a sexist binary system was difficult. As social discourse changed to allow more gender categories, they were able to find a gender expression such as "they" to express their non-binary sense of self.

5.4 Visibility

Many personal writings of trans individuals give voice to a sense of isolation. Feeling born into the wrong body, the trans individual can also feel that he, she, or they has few compatriots. Being able to read the personal writings of similar others may help diminish the sense of isolation. It may be helpful to trans individuals to know where their experiences echo those of other trans folk and where they diverge. Despite the presumably great diversity of experiences, attitudes, and feelings among transgendered people, some basic issues – the search for the true self, the distinction between a deep reality and what appears on the surface, the challenges of affirmation – appear to run through most accounts.

It is not only trans individuals who benefit from learning about the life experiences of those who are not content with the gender assigned to them at birth; caring cis individuals also benefit. To anyone who has struggled with any form of isolation, with any questions about the self, seeing the honest struggles of others can be an inspiration – especially when the struggles have led to greater and greater social acceptance.

And, as we have said before, everyone – cis or trans – may experience growth by rethinking something that has seemed so "fixed" as the concept of gender. Some trans individuals see themselves not so much un-doing the gender binary as re-doing the gender binary while others see themselves as un-doing the binary. But whatever the approach, any prolonged contemplation of the lived experiences of transgendered people brings us face to face with the complexities and fluidity of gender.

6 Social Scientific Studies of Rejection and Acceptance

Self-revealing accounts by public figures give us a sense of the experiences of trans individuals. But compelling as they are, the accounts are necessarily limited. Learning about the experiences of famous people leaves us wondering if the experiences of less famous people, ordinary people, would be similar. First-hand accounts, furthermore, are necessarily incomplete because they tend not to provide as much social context as we need for a full understanding.

To complete our understanding, we must turn to social scientific studies. Social scientists distinguish between attitudes, on the one hand, and behaviors, on the other. Attitudes are a mixture of thoughts and feelings, while behaviors are actions. Often there is a close connection between attitudes and behaviors – as when a prejudiced person acts in discriminatory ways toward the objects of their dislike. Yet, the relationship between attitudes and behaviors is a lot less direct and simple than you might think. Social systems can be set up in a way that disrupts this relationship. Sometimes, busy people are simply doing what is easiest for them to do within a given social system without paying attention to the consequences for others; but the results might be very harmful for those whose lives and needs do not fit into the prescribed systems. When institutions have been set up in the past by prejudiced people, today's busy people may thus cause harm – quite unintentionally – simply by adhering to the seemingly bland and nondiscriminatory rules of the institution. This is called structural discrimination. On the other side of the coin, systems can sometimes prevent those who are filled with negative feelings from expressing their wrath. Sometimes systems are set up to favor the actions of fair-minded, thoughtful, and inclusive people.

Social scientific research shows how societal stigma colors the lived experiences of transgender individuals. Echoing the memories of public figures, the statistics found through systematic and painstaking research show that the cards are generally stacked against trans people. Structural discriminations include the ways in which transgender accesses to resources, services, and rights, are obstructed by bureaucratic systems and individuals in professional roles. The major structural stigmas faced by transgender people are housing and employment discrimination as well as increased policing and incarceration. Although much has changed in recent years, the medical profession has pathologized transgender identity and transgender experiences.

Research also suggests ways to improve the situation. Some think that support starts with understanding. Accurate information can help build compassion and also can suggest aspects of the social environment that need can be changed for the better.

6.1 Housing Discrimination

An important component of the structural stigma faced by transgender people is based in housing discrimination. A home in which one feels safe is a basic human need. Transgender people often find it hard to obtain and secure a home to live in. Several surveys suggest that housing discrimination is common. For instance, a survey of 6,450 transgender or nonbinary people who were recruited from online transgender list servs and local communities in the US, found that approximately one in five transgender people were denied a home or apartment (Grant et al., 2011). Moreover, one in five of this sample reported becoming homeless because of their transgender status. African American survey participants were over three times as likely to become homeless as the rest of the population (Kattari et al., 2016). The largest survey of transgender people thus far, the US Transgender Survey (USTS) of 2015, also reports a high percentage of housing discrimination. This survey, although based on a convenience sample recruited from listservs and transgender communities all over the United States, is currently one of the best ways to assess rates of discrimination because the Census Bureau survey (which surveys 3.5 million households each year) does not ask respondents to indicate if they identify as transgender people. The USTS included 27,715 transgender and nonbinary-identified individuals recruited from all over the United States. About 23 percent of participants reported being evicted or denied a home or an apartment because they were transgender. About one-third of respondents experienced homelessness at some point in their lives (James et al., 2016).

Moving away from self-report surveys of transgender people, researchers compared transgender and nontransgender pairs as they applied for housing in the Boston area. The matched pairs included a transgender or gender nonconforming tester with a gender-conforming tester ("controls"). The matched pair renter profiles were similar, and they both contacted randomly selected property owners who were advertising apartments. Early in the process, transgender applicants indicated that they were gender nonbinary or transgender by indicating that their pronouns were "they/them" or that their name would be different in the credit check. Following the showing of the apartment, each tester wrote a report about their visit to the apartment. The matched pairs never met one another, and thirty-three such pairs were used in the study. The result show that 61 percent of the time transgender and gender-nonconforming people tended to receive discriminatory treatment. Trans testers were 21 percent less likely to be afforded financial incentives to rent than were the comparisons. They were 12 percent more likely to be given negative information about the apartment. They were 9 percent more likely to be quoted a higher rental price (Langowski et al., 2017). Although not all of the differences were statistically significant, the results show that 61 percent of the time transgender and gender-nonconforming people tended to receive discriminatory treatment.

Housing discrimination, social rejection, and economic insecurity have been associated with high levels of homelessness among transgender people (Cruz, 2011). Various surveys based on convenience samples suggest that rates of homelessness range from 20–30 percent (Grant et al., 2011; James et al., 2016; these rates are high compared to the general population. Transgender and other LGBQI+ are estimated to encompass 20–40 percent of the 1.6 million homeless youth in the United States (transequality.org, n.d.). About 70 percent of those who stayed in a shelter reported some form of harassment or discrimination (James et al., 2016).

A qualitative study examining the experiences of transgender women and two-spirit people seeking homeless shelters in Vancouver, British Colombia, also showed that gender nonconforming people are discriminated against in shelters. One woman described her experience living in supported services: "When I first lived at [supported housing] there was some woman that disrespected me in every way, [saying] I shouldn't be there, I have no right being there and they were gonna sign a petition for us trans people not to live there" (Lyons et al., 2016, p. 375).

6.2 Employment Discrimination

Employment discrimination creates multiple jeopardies because it leads to suffering on a regular basis, and it also decreases transgender people's chances of economic independence. Jessi Dye, for instance, was called in to her supervisor's office and was asked, "What are you?" Ms. Dye explained that she was a transgender woman in transition. Her supervisor asked how she could employ a person that "looked one way" but was "another way." Jessi Dye was later fired from her position in the nursing home (Katri, 2017).

A national survey of transgender people reports that approximately 90 percent have experienced discrimination at work (Grant et al., 2011). In studies conducted between 1996 and 2006, 20–57 percent reported having experienced employment discrimination at some point in their lives; 13–56 percent were fired, 13–47 percent were denied employment, 22–31 percent were harassed, and 19 percent were denied promotion (Badgett et al., 2007). In 2015, the USTS reported that 15 percent of those who answered the survey were unemployed, which was three time higher than the 5 percent unemployment rate in the US population at the time. One in six transgender workers who responded to the USTS said they lost a job because of their transgender status. Fifteen percent of those who had a job reported being verbally harassed, physically attacked, and sexually assaulted at work because of their transgender or nonbinary identity (James et al., 2016).

Some transgender employees face physical threats and emotional abuse. Abuse includes being confronted with their assigned gender at birth, not being able to use a restroom that matches one's identity, or having a boss or a coworker disclose private information about one's transgender status. In the USTS sample, one in six (16 percent) said that, because they were transgender, a boss or coworker shared personal information about them that should not have been shared. Six percent said that their boss gave them a negative review because they were transgender, 4 percent were told to present in the wrong gender in order to keep their job, and 4 percent said that they were not allowed to use the restroom consistent with their gender identity (James et al., 2016, p. 153).

Sometimes negativity in the work environment is more covert than blatant. Experiences of micro-aggression at work are common. An encounter can appear rather neutral but be very emotionally charged as, for example, when transgender people must submit to receiving advice from cisgender people on how to appear and act more like a "woman" or a "man"(Brewster et al., 2014). Disenfranchisement in the workplace results in high levels of poverty among transgender people. Transgender workers are almost four times more likely to report a household income of under $10,000 (Human Rights Campaign staff, 2013, September 6) compared to the general population. One third of transgender people who responded to the USTS reported living in poverty (James et al., 2016).

Poverty and discrimination result in high levels of participation in the underground economy, including sex work (Badgett et al., 2007; Grant et al., 2011; James et al., 2016). USTS found that one in five respondents participated in sex work, drug sales, and other forms of work that is criminalized (James et al., 2016). Consequently, a high number of transgender people are incarcerated in the United States. USTS reports that almost one in six of the survey respondents were incarcerated and one in two black transgender people spent time beyond bars.

6.3 Discrimination in the Justice System

As if other forms of discrimination were not enough, the American legal system seems to perpetuate discrimination. Kuvalanka, Bellis, Goldberg, and McGuire (2019) published a revealing article about their in-depth interviews of ten mothers of gender non-conforming children who were caught in custody battles for the children. The children ranged in age from five to fifteen. Bias on the part of the judges and others in the legal system emerged as a major theme of the interviews. Essentially, the women were punished by the legal system for affirming the identities of their children. The 2019 findings of Kuvalanka et al. were in line with previous analyses (Ehrensaft, 2011; Margolis, 2016; Perkiss, 2014; Skougard, 2011).

Research on the experiences of transgender adults also shows discrimination. Trans individuals, particularly trans women, are profiled and harassed by police more frequently than one would expect by chance alone (Carpenter & Marshall, 2017). An Amnesty International report found that transgender women are sometimes closely scrutinized by police and often profiled as sex workers. Even when a transgender woman is doing a commonplace daily activity like walking to a local shop, she is at risk of being profiled as a sex worker (Amnesty International, 2016). This sort of profiling by police is called "walking while trans," and contributes to the high rates of incarceration of transgender women. The situation can deteriorate rapidly. Mistrust of the legal system leads many transgender women to miss their hearing dates. Those apprehended then seem to fail to address citations issued when "walking while trans" (or for no apparent criminal activity). As a result of not addressing bench warrants out for arrest, what begins as a minor incident can continue as a traumatic journey into the prison system (Carpenter & Marshall, 2017).

When transgender people are arrested, they enter one of the most gender-binary institutions: the prison. As they enter prison, many transgender people are assigned to a facility based on their assigned gender at birth. This leads transgender women who live, act, and identify as women to be put in a men's prison. Reports suggest that transgender women face extreme abuse and harassment in men's facilities from both inmates and correctional officers. Their gender nonconformity makes transgender women a moving target. One transgender woman reported, "I am raped on a daily basis, I've made complaints but no response. No success. I'm scared to push forward with my complaint against officers for beating me and raping me" (Faithful, 2009, p. 3). Rapes in jail can serve as a death sentence as they increase inmates' chances of contracting incurable sexually transmitted diseases like HIV – which, in the context of the US prison system, is rarely adequately treated with the best available medicines.

To protect transgender inmates and sustain order in the facilities, prison officials sometimes move transgender inmates to isolated cells. Instead of punishing cisgender aggressors, officials sometimes put transgender inmates in isolation for up to twenty-three hours a day. Some report feeling safe in isolation, but other transgender inmates feel less safe when the lack of security cameras makes them more vulnerable to abuse by guards (The Sylvia Rivera Law Project, 2007).

In addition to physical abuse, transgender inmates also experience psychological abuse in prison. Isolated confinements, strip searches, forced gender conformity, and disregard to their identity are traumatic experiences confronted by transgender inmates (Malkin & DeJong, 2018).

Especially difficult for many inmates on the trans spectrum is the lack of access to hormonal therapies. Estimations suggest that transgender inmates with gender dysphoria who seek transition may encompass fewer than 1,000 people in the USA; nevertheless, their medical and custodial needs are substantial (Brown, 2014). When transgender people who seek transition lack access to hormones this may result in depression, shame, and emotional instability. It may also result in self-harming, and, in extreme cases, auto-castration and auto-penectomy (Brown, 2010; Sevelius & Jenness, 2017).

A content analysis of letters sent to researchers who began a pen-pal communication with twenty-three transgender inmates suggests that access to hormones was a significant concern. A participant named Amanda wrote, "I'm depressed most of the time, not being able to express my true self and still being in the wrong body, not being comfortable in my appearance. I have crying fits often for no reason, and I forgo eating so I won't have to be around other people because I'm ashamed of my looks" (Rosenberg & Oswin, 2015, p. 1277). Another participant wrote, "You tend to get depressed because you see your body reversing to what you don't want it to be. My breasts have become somewhat hard and my features are not like I would want them to be on hormones. Everything that I have worked for so I can have surgery has gone down the drain" (Rosenberg & Oswin, 2015, p. 1277).

Another study showed similarly distressing results. Analyzing 129 unsolicited letters sent by prisoners to a *Trans in Prison* journal suggests strong concern with health care issues for trans prisoners. Five percent of the sample reported that they attempted or completed auto-castration in prison. For instance, one prisoner wrote, "I castrated myself after giving up at the time on receiving treatment with hormones after many years" (Brown, 2014, p. 337). Prisoners who self-castrate in prison are hospitalized and require numerous transfusions and surgical interventions (Brown, 2010).

6.4 Prejudice and Discrimination in Psychiatric Medicine

A final source of stigma that has been used to assist but also to pathologize transgender people is the medicalization of their identity. Psychology and psychiatry often tout liberation. Yet both fields have been reactionary and

repressive in how they approach transgender people. Both fields have traditionally distanced themselves from transgender people and from real understanding
through the pathologizing of transgender disposition. One way to attempt to
neutralize transgender people is to call them mentally ill. Framing transgender
people as mentally ill was a prevalent response in a research survey from
countries around the globe including China, Malaysia, Singapore, Thailand,
Philippines, United Kingdom, and the United States (Winter, Webster, &
Cheung, 2008).

According to psychologists and psychiatrists, feelings, thoughts, and actions
that cause distress or impair good functioning are conceptualized as disorders.
Bundles of feelings, thoughts, and actions that form certain patterns are categorized in the Diagnostic and Statistical Manual or DSM, published by the
American Psychiatric Association (APA). The DSM goes through periodic
revisions. Patterns that were classified as problematic in one era may be dropped
from the DSM in another era. In 1973, the APA dropped homosexuality from
the DSM II. Previously, homosexuality was classified as a disorder.

With homosexuality out of the DSM-III, Transsexualism and Gender Identity
Disorder in Childhood (GIDC) were added to its list of mental disorders. In the
DSM-IV, transsexualism was modified to include Gender Identity Disorder in
adults and adolescents (GID). The diagnostic criteria for gender identity disorder are:

> A. Strong and persistent cross-gender identification (not merely a desire for
> any perceived cultural advantages of being the other sex). In children, the
> disturbance is manifested by four (or more) of the following: 1. repeatedly
> stated desire to be, or insistence that he or she is, the other sex, 2. in boys,
> preference for cross-dressing or simulating female attire; in girls, insistence
> on wearing only stereotypical masculine clothing. 3. strong and persistent
> preferences for cross-sex roles in make-believe play or persistent fantasies of
> being the other sex. 4. intense desire to participate in the stereotypical games
> and pastimes of the other sex. 5. strong preference for playmates of the other
> sex.
>
> Persistent discomfort with his or her sex or sense of inappropriateness in
> the gender role of that sex.
>
> The disturbance is not concurrent with a physical intersex condition.
>
> The disturbance causes clinically significant distress or impairment in
> social, occupational, or other important areas of functioning (American
> Psychiatric Association, 2000).

Activists protesting the GID diagnosis argued that the diagnosis contributed to
pathologizing of gender-variant individuals (Burke, 2011; Davy, 2015; Lev,
2006, 2013b). Moreover, many activists were concerned that the GID criteria
reinforced the premise that all people should arrive on the planet in one of two

essential genders (Burke, 2011). The GID category assumes that gender conformity is the norm; gender nonconformity becomes, ipso facto, abnormal. Serano (2009, June 12) concludes, "After all, so long as any form of gender variance is codified in the pages of the DSM, it will continue to be cited by trans-invalidators as evidence that we are mentally inferior and incompetent" (p. 7).

In 2008, the APA announced a task force for updating the DSM manual. In 2010, the APA released a draft proposal for the DSM-V. In this draft, Gender Identity Disorder was changed to Gender Incongruence. The taskforce reasoned that Gender Incongruence is a descriptive term that does not stigmatize in the same manner that Gender Identity Disorder does. Indeed, many welcomed the dropping of the disorder suffix from the medical category (Kamens, 2011). Eventually, with the involvement of the World Professional Association for Transgender Health (WPATH), the word "incongruence" was replaced with the word "dysphoria" (De Cuypere, Knudson, & Bockting, 2010).

In 2013, the APA published the DSM-5. It replaced GID with the new diagnosis Gender Dysphoria in both adults and children. The DSM-5 identifies gender dysphoria in adolescents and adults as a noticeable mismatch between the gender the person feels they are and the gender society understands them to be. This disparity should be ongoing for at least six months and should involve a strong distress that affects individuals socially, at work, or in other important parts of their life (Zucker, 2015b).

Jack Drescher (2014) belonged to both the American Psychiatric Association and the World Health Organization (WHO) and served on the committees of both organizations that created their manuals, the DSM-V and the International Classification of Diseases, respectively. Drescher described the essential conundrum for both committees: To gain care, people need to be diagnosed as ill (Drescher, 2014). So, in the process of trying to improve lives for transgender people, the medical professions can cause harmful side-effects through the dynamics of stigma (Davy, 2010, 2015).

The difficulties continue as treatment continues, especially for those seeking hormone therapy or surgical procedures. For instance, Spade (2003) noted that approval of his request for surgery rested on counselors seeing him as having a "commitment to 'full-time' maleness, or they can't be sure that I won't regret my surgery. ... [T]hat I don't want to change my first name, that I haven't sought out the use of the pronoun 'he,' that I don't think that 'lesbian' is the wrong word for me ... is my undoing" (Spade, 2003; p. 21). Although cisgender people are not expected to always embody masculinity or femininity (Bem, 1993; Serano, 2009), transgender patients are required to desire to and conform to the stereotypical behavior of the opposite sex in order to receive all the treatments they wish (Davy, 2015).

Medicalization verses Stigma. Another important challenge to the medicalization of transgender identity is the increased attention to research that shows that transgender people do not inherently experience torment and suffering because of the incongruence between certain dimensions in their gender identity; rather, it is stress from the environment that creates torment and suffering. In an important study, Robles et al. (2016), asked if distress related to the social consequences of gender nonconformity (e.g., stigmatization) can be distinguished from psychological distress related to transgender identity. To answer this question the researcher conducted structured interviews with 250 transgender-identified individuals receiving healthcare services from Condesa Specialised Clinic in Mexico City. Eighty-one percent of the sample were transfeminine. Participants tended to report first being aware of their transgender identity at a mean age of 5.6. The large majority – 74 percent – used hormones or surgery to change their appearance (Robles et al., 2016).

In these studies, interviewers asked the participants questions that covered the diagnostic elements of the gender incongruence. Participants were also asked about social rejection and violence; including family rejection, sexual violence, and rejection by schoolmates or coworkers. Coding interviewees' responses, researchers then conducted a regression analysis and found that variance in psychological distress associated with being transgender was predicted by family rejection, school/workmate rejection, physical violence, sexual violence, and psychological harassment and violence. The researchers interpret the findings as suggesting that the psychological distress of being transgender is not an inherent feature of transgender identity but rather that social stigma and marginalization are key contributors to the psychological distress of being transgender (Robles et al., 2016).

6.5 Transphobic Beliefs

From studies about the lived experiences of trans women and men, and especially from studies about how trans people face discrimination, it seems logical to conclude that many individuals in society are prejudiced against transgender humans. When the prejudice is really deep, it becomes transphobia or fear (often unacknowledged at a conscious level) of transgender people and of transsexuality.

Understanding anti-trans prejudice and discrimination starts by documenting its properties, noting how common it is, how it spreads, and how it can be transformed or contained. The seemingly simple task of documentation is, however, complicated by the phenomenon itself. It's hard to map the universe when the lens of the telescope is warped. It's difficult to document prejudice when the researchers are, themselves, prejudiced.

What about the rest of society, those who have not gone to medical school and do not practice medicine? What do studies reveal about the feelings, attitudes, or opinions of average citizens? Flores, Miller, and Tadlock (2018) report on three studies conducted in 2015 and 2016 in which national probability samples of approximately 1,000 to 2,000 were surveyed (in each survey). The researcher assessed feelings toward transgender people in comparison to other groups in American society. Participants were asked to rate a number of groups on a scale in which 100 indicate very warm feelings and 0 colder or less favorable feelings. Participants were also asked the extent to which they saw transgender people as moral, and the extent to which they supported equal rights protection (e.g., protection from discrimination in the workplace).

The findings indicated that transgender people received a score of around 46 on the warmth thermometer. They were seen in more negative light than gun owners, gay men, and lesbian women, and in a more positive light than fundamentalist Christians, Democrats, and rich people. In terms of seeing transgender people as moral, Americans were almost evenly divided: 37–39 percent did not believe that transgender expression or sex change are morally wrong; 29–32 percent neither agreed nor disagreed; and 29–34 percent agreed with statements that frame transgender people as immoral.

Finally, in terms of polices, the research indicates relatively higher levels of support for transgender rights compared to warmth toward transgender people. About 61 percent of the respondent agreed that transgender people deserve the same rights and protections as other Americans, 30 percent were neutral, and 9 percent disagreed.

A 2017 survey conducted in different countries using a sample drawn from panels of participants (approximately 1,000 from each country) suggests that in many countries there is openness toward acceptance of transgender people. Acceptance is related to decreases in transphobia, increases in positive beliefs about transgender people, increases in support for transgender rights (Ipsos, 2017 January 29). The survey indicated that about 32 percent of Americans somewhat or strongly agree with statements that framed transgender people in transphobic terms; as mentally ill or committing a sin. Countries with less transphobic respondents included Spain where only 9 percent agreed/somewhat agreed with statements that framed transgender people as mentally ill, followed by Italy (11 percent), Argentina (13 percent), France (13 percent), and Great Britain (13 percent). In turn, in the United States, 57 percent agreed or some-what agreed with statements that framed transgender people as brave, compared to 74 percent in Spain, 70 percent in Argentina, 69 percent in Great Britain,

67 percent in Sweden, 66 percent in Germany, and 65 percent in both Canada and Italy. Lower agreement with the framing of transgender people as brave was found in Hungary (48 percent), South Korea (48 percent), and Japan (38 percent) (Ipsos, 2017 January 29).

A survey study done in collaboration with the Williams Institute at UCLA and Buzzfeed examined support for pro-transgender policy in different parts of the world. This research was a panel-based survey in countries with relatively high Internet use. Samples from each panel included approximately 1,000 people. Questions assessing policy support included: do you believe that transgender people need to be protected from discrimination by the government; do you believe that transgender people should be allowed to use the restroom of the sex they identify with; and do you believe that transgender people should be allowed to adopt children. The United States ranked tenth in terms of support for transgender equality, with Spain (1st), Sweden (2nd), Argentina (3rd), Canada (4th), Germany (5th), United Kingdom (6th), Belgium (7th), India (8th), and Australia (9th) ranking above it. Lower levels of support for transgender equal rights were found in Russia (16th from the bottom), Hungary (15th), South Korea (14th), and Poland (13th). Moreover, when participants were asked "what do you believe should be required before a transgender person can legally change their sex on identity documents, such as government ID cards or driving license?", the United States together with South Korea had the highest percentage of respondents (24 percent) say "changes to legal sex should not be allowed no matter what" (Lester Feder, Singer-Vine, King, 2016, December 29).

Researchers also found that people perceive their countries as becoming more tolerant toward transgender people, with 78 percent agreement in Argentina, 73 percent in Sweden, 71 percent in Australia, and 71 percent in the United State. People in Hungary (31 percent), Poland (41 percent), and Japan (43 percent) were least likely to see their nation as more tolerant of transgender people (Ipsos, 2017). A 2017 Pew Survey reported that 39 percent of Americans believe that society has not gone far enough when it comes to accepting people who are transgender, 27 percent say that society has been about right in accepting transgender people, and 32 percent people believe that society has gone too far (Pew, 2017).

Transphobia (seeing trans people as immoral or unnatural) occurs more often among men than among women (Winter et al., 2008). In survey samples from the United Kingdom, Canada, Poland, the United States, Sweden and Hong Kong, male students were found to be more prejudiced than female students against transgender people (Nagoshi et al., 2008; Norton & Herek, 2013; Tebbe & Moradi, 2012; Winter et al., 2008), and more likely to oppose their civil rights (Antoszewski et al., 2007; Landén & Innala, 2000; Tee &

Hegarty, 2006). Worthen (2016) found that the gender difference in attitudes was not simply a function of attitudes toward LGB populations. That is, at any given spot on the pro- or anti-gay rights spectrum, men still seem to be more anti-transgender than women are, even after controlling for pro-LGB attitudes and feminist attitudes.

Why is transphobia greater among men than among women? Some speculate that men have a greater investment than women in hierarchy. Men's negative attitudes toward transgender people could be the result of fear of losing their dominant position in society. When other men perform in a feminine way, fearful men might cling to their dominance (Harrison & Michelson, 2019; Warriner, Nagoshi, & Nagoshi, 2013).

6.5.1 Correlates of Anti-transgender Attitudes

A deeper examination of the content of anti-transgender attitudes suggests that it is based on the gender rebel idea. This explanation postulates that because transgender people transgress essentialist and binary notions of gender they are hated and are discriminated against (Adams et al., 2017). Among the assumptions that transgender people transgress is that there are only two genders, and that these genders are determined by biological genitals. Another assumption transgressed by transgender people is that gender is invariant. Because transgender people do not satisfy these assumptions, they are either not taken seriously or they are pathologized.

Binary Gender Norms. There is much empirical evidence to support the postulation that transprejudice and transphobia are associated with a belief in binary gender. An experimental study in China indicates that when individuals are primed to think about gender as grounded in neurobiological processes, compared to an interaction between neurobiology and the environment, they are more likely to express transphobic attitudes (Ching & Xu, 2018). A large research study with a national probability sample of Americans demonstrates that binary conceptions of gender are negatively associated with warmth and positive attitudes toward transgender people (Norton & Herek, 2013; also Tee & Hegarty, 2006, with a smaller UK sample). In addition, researchers have found that strong adherence to masculine norms among male-identified students strongly correlated with transphobia (Watjen & Mitchell, 2013). Hostile sexism (in which women are objectified and degraded) is also associated with transphobia (Nagoshi et al., 2008), as is benevolent sexism (in which women are idealized as wives, mothers, and daughters) (Harrison & Michelson, 2019; Warriner et al., 2013).

Conservative Attitudes. Certainly, there is a strong connection among both women and men between a need for strong authority, on the one hand, and a rejection of equality, on the other. People who exhibit a lot of conservatism and religiosity tend to also manifest transgender prejudice (Elischberger et al., 2018; Miller et al., 2017; Nagoshi et al., 2008; Norton & Herek, 2013; Peterson & Zurbriggen, 2010; Taylor, Haider-Markel, & Lewis, 2018). Moreover, Garelick et al., (2017) found that individual differences in the extent to which a person fears being wrong (i.e., invalidated) were associated with increased rejection of transgender and bisexual people – but not of gays and lesbians. The authors explained that since bisexuality challenges the sexual binary and trans identity may challenge the gender binary, people whose cognitive processing includes a fear of being invalidated and a strong need to correctly categorize people were more likely to reject transgender and bisexual people but not gays and lesbians (Garelick et al., 2017). Related to conservative beliefs, self-identification as religious or as Christian (and to a lesser extent as being Muslim) is associated with anti-transgender attitudes. Strong predictors for anti-transgender attitudes among religious people were religious fundamentalism, high frequency of church attendance, and literal interpretation of biblical texts (Campbell, Hinton, & Anderson, 2019).

Homophobia and Transphobia. Research suggests that there is a relationship between transprejudice and homophobia (Nagoshi et al., 2008; Norton & Herek, 2013; Tee & Hegarty, 2006). Despite this association, lesbians and gay men can also express prejudice against transgender people (Warriner et al., 2013). Particularly interesting is a study conducted by Wang-Jones, Hauson, Ferdman, Hattrup, & Lowman, 2018, who reasoned that people who have exclusive same-sex attraction (e.g., lesbian or gay) or exclusive other-gender attraction (i.e., heterosexual) were more likely to have implicit bias against transgender people compared to individuals whose sexual attraction is not targeted at a specific gender. Current categories for people who are not attracted to a specific gender category include bisexual, pansexual (i.e., omnisexuality in which people are attracted to others regardless of their sex or gender), and asexual (low or lack of desire for sexual activity). For the Wang-Jones et al. study, the researchers recruited 54 gay, 79 straight, and 132 non-monosexuals (i.e., pansexual, bisexual, and asexual people) to participate in an online study. They gave them measures of explicit attitudes toward transgender people; for instance, to rate on a 0–100 scale their sense of warmth toward trans men and trans women. They also gave participants an implicit measure in which the participants were asked to match words such as marvelous, pleasure, beautiful, horrible, painful, nasty, and tragic with transsexual women, "biological women," transsexual men, and "biological men." The study showed that although gay men had explicit positive attitudes toward trans women and men, gay men took longer to match positive words with transgender men and women compared to cisgender men and women, suggesting implicit bias. All groups, regardless of sexual orientation, had negative implicit attitudes toward trans women.

6.5.2 Predictors for Positive Attitudes toward Transgender People

More tolerant attitudes toward transgender people are associated with lower levels of religiosity, liberal political attitudes, and higher levels of education. Some contextual factors also play an important role in reducing prejudice toward transgender people (Flores, Miller, & Tadlock, 2018).

Contact. One of the key contextual factors associated with reduction in transphobia is contact with transgender people. As is the case with attitudes toward other minority groups, researchers find that contact, acquaintance, and friendship with transgender people is associated with less prejudice toward them. Survey studies consistently suggest that people who know a transgender person are less likely than others to rate or frame transgender people in unfavorable terms (Flores et al., 2018; Norton & Herek, 2013; Tadlock et al., 2017). Studies also indicate that because the transgender population is relatively small, many Americans are unlikely to indicate knowing a transgender person. Fortunately, positive attitudes toward lesbians and gays tend to generalize to transgender people (Flores, 2015).

Engagement with life stories and narratives by and of transgender people is also correlated with reduction in prejudice. The Internet in particular has afforded many channels in which transgender people can document their lives, including their emotions and their thoughts. Many video blogs online document the subjective process of transitioning. These personal videos on online platforms such as YouTube and Tumblr allow transgender people to create a sense of community that share their stories and experiences (Miller, 2017).

From the family studies literature, Kuvalanka and colleagues have focused on caregivers (including at schools), showing that support makes a positive impact for trans-spectrum youth (e.g., Kuvalanka et al., 2017). Similarly, McGuire et al., (2016) have argued that having a trans-spectrum family member impacts gender development within families in a positive way – helping all family members expand their ideas about gender (see also Olson & Enright, 2018).

Perspective-Taking. Public exposure to the transgender experience in online videos, webinars, television shows, and films can play an important role in reducing transgender prejudice (Mizock et al., 2017). For instance, Gillig,

Rosenthal, Murphy, and Langrall Folb (2017) recruited participants from social media sites of the show *Royal Pains* that focuses on the life of an on-call doctor in the Hamptons. One episode depicted the struggles of a transgender teenager. Gillig et al., (2017) found that the more a viewer took the perspective of the teenager, the less likely they were to hold anti-trans attitudes. Moreover, viewers who consumed other shows with transgender representation such as Laverne Cox's *Orange Is the New Black* were also less likely to hold anti-trans beliefs than were comparison groups (Gillig et al., 2017).

Conversations that enhance perspective-taking also chip away at transphobia. In a field experiment conducted in South Florida, canvassers went door to door and engaged people in a brief interaction concerning recycling or transgender issues. Households were randomly assigned to one condition or the other. Thus, half of the households were given information about transgender people and shown a short video. They were then asked by the canvasser to think of a time in their life in which they were judged negatively for being different. They were then asked to explain how their own experience offered a window to the discrimination and prejudice against transgender people. The comparison group in this study was households who engaged in conversation about recycling.

Members of the different households took a survey before and after their participation in the study. Comparison of their responses suggest that the perspective-taking intervention worked to reduce prejudice toward transgender people and increase support for policies that protect transgender rights (Broockman & Kalla, 2016).

7 Reflections and Parting Wishes

Whenever we deal with human behavior, we are prone to leave the realm of pure objectivity and veer toward subjectivity. Objective information is information that appears the same to different people, no matter what their backgrounds or their agendas. Thus, if you measure the height of your son as six feet tall and your political opponent measures the height of your son as six feet tall, you agree: objectively, the fellow is six feet tall. Some information is subjective, not objective. You might declare that your son is a compassionate and loving person; but his ex-spouse might disagree. The disagreement shows the information to lack objectivity.

As researchers in the field of gender studies, we have tried our best to present information that is objectively true about the experiences of transgender people. We have presented current thinking of biologists about the human body and have reported on carefully conducted studies. We have also offered numerous conceptualizations that have allowed us to group the objective information into meaningful units.

We have not, however, pretended to be neutral. As Crosby and Bearman (2006) have noted, social scientific researchers too often confound objectivity and neutrality. The conviction that one can derive conclusions about what is good behavior or what constitutes good social arrangements on the basis of objective data is a false conviction; but it is also false to imagine that we must discard our human values whenever we rely on objective information.

Without apology, we declare that we wish good lives for all people, trans or cis. We take as self-evident the truth that all people have the need and the right to live in a world in which they are valued and respected. These feminist principles offer the basis for deciding how to use the objective data that we encounter. We also hold that knowledge helps build respect. It may be hard for most cis people to walk in the shoes of transgender people, metaphorically speaking, but empathy may at least be built through increased knowledge and understanding of the paths taken.

7.1 Transgender Liberation

Great strides toward transgender liberation occurred in the 1960 and 1970s. Some of the key events were spontaneous acts of collective resistance to harassment in commercial establishments (e.g., bars and cafeterias) in major urban centers like Los Angeles, Philadelphia, and New York. During some riots, transgender people rose up against police brutality and harassment. For instance, in an event documented by the film *Screaming Queens: The Riot at Compton's Cafeteria* (2005), Susan Stryker and Victor Silverman describe the riot at the Compton's Cafeteria in San Francisco's Tenderloin district in 1966 (Stryker & Silverman, 2005). The Compton's Cafeteria riot was the first collective act of militant resistance by transgender women and drag queens fighting against police brutality. The collective action by the "queens" of the tenderloin strengthened the emerging transgender liberation movement that sought better treatment from the police, medical providers, city government, and state government.

The 1990s have been said to mark the beginning of a more accepting period for transgender people. Media coverage, scholarship, and art depicting the transgender experience gain more permanency after the long period of LGBTQI+ marginalization due to the AIDS scare.

Among the important transgender activists and educators of the time were Kate Bornstein, author of *Gender Outlaw* (1994). Activist Lesley Feinberg's 1992 manifesto *Transgender Liberation: A Movement Whose Time Has Come* energized transgender activists and their allies. LGB organizations added T to their names (Stryker, 2008b). Trans-masculine photographer Loren Cameron's book *Body Alchemy* increased the visibility of trans male bodies. The musician Anohni, the lead singer in the band Antony and the Johnsons, highlighted transgender experiences in their music (see Stryker, 2008a for details).

The first two decades of the millennium have been a tipping point in the ways American society understands transgender people (Steinmetz, 2014). During this time, transgender figures gained mainstream visibility that didn't sensationalize their identity as in previous decades, but increasingly respected and celebrated them. Educators, parents, and their children have been exposed to celebrity narratives that helped create a better understanding of the transgender experience.

7.2 Concepts to Continue the Liberation

We propose that two simple concepts may allow us all to help advance toward the goal of enhanced acceptance. First, people benefit from being the ones to define themselves. Second, we can see people as falling into categories and we can also see people as a bundle of characteristics.

Labeling Others and Labeling the Self. First, consider that when we see the world, we are in the subjective mode and those whom we see are objects in our perception. They may be perceptual objects with sentience and volition, unlike inanimate objects; but they are perceptual objects nonetheless. Sometimes we are the perceptual objects in the view of others. And sometimes, when we reflect on ourselves, we are both subject and object.

Humans live in groups. Some groups have the privilege of setting the terms in which the world is seen. They pick the labels. Of course, privileges entail responsibilities too, and sometimes the dominant group self-consciously embraces what it sees as its responsibilities while enjoying its privileges.

When physicians label newborns, announcing that a child is either a girl or a boy, they take seriously their professional responsibilities and their responsibilities as cultural authorities and caregivers. They simultaneously exercise privileges. When the parent or parents repeat the label and augment it, they too fulfill responsibilities and exercise authority. If the child feels the label does not fit, then the child's subjective sense of self is at loggerheads with what the society has created as the perceptual object.

It is difficult, but important, to remember that how you see another may not be how the other experiences herself, himself, or themself. For years, one of the authors had seen her relative as a girl. In recent times, after the transition, the author found out that the person she saw as a girl had always thought of herself, privately, as a boy. Now when the author recounts a family story about the relative as a child, the author refers to the relative as a boy and uses the relative's affirmed name – which was not the name used years ago.

A rallying cry of many in trans communities is this: let us determine our identities. When you define our identities, you assert your right as master. We would rather be masters of ourselves. Salience also matters. At this exact moment, you might be looking at the three authors as women; but while working we might be conscious only of being feminist academic writers. We might all be on the same page about perceived and experienced gender, but while you might be focused on our gender, our womanhood may not be the most important characteristic of ourselves as we sit and write. Thus, what is salient about each of us to herself may not be what is in the minds of others at the moment that they encounter us.

A rallying cry for most feminists – trans or cis – is this: at any one moment, let us determine what is salient. At some precise moment, somewhere you might find two people for whom gender of the self and gender of the other is extremely salient and who, at that very moment, both wish to express their feelings sexually. But at other moments, the salience of gender might exist for only one of the people in the pair; if that gender-conscious person makes sexual advances, the other person may be surprised. If the gender-conscious person persists, the result is harassment.

Characteristics, Not Categories. Also useful is the distinction between categories and characteristics. For the sake of linguistic convenience, we often put individuals into categories. Sometimes the categories are divided into two subcategories. People might be seen as old or young, short or tall, male or female. Sometimes the categories have multiple subdivisions. People might, for example, be seen as infants, toddlers, children, adolescents, young adults, middle-age, old, or very old.

When we think of people in categories, other dimensions of their being fall away. We might, for example, see age as the only characteristic about a person that matters in some situations. Other aspects of the person are momentarily irrelevant. The phenomenon has been called "essentializing."

In the early days of feminist social science, during the late 1960s and 1970s, when the great debates raged over the degree of differences between females and males (Eagly, 2018; Hyde, 2005; Maccoby & Jacklin, 1974), some scholars noted that the result was to essentialize gender (Crosby & Wyche, 1996). Differences among women – due to ethnicity, sexual orientation, class, age, and so on – evaporated and so did differences among men as the academic battles centered around the supposed and contested differences between women and men.

We can shift our perspective. We can think of every human as having characteristics. Some of these characteristics are shared by all living humans. Some characteristics are shared by many other living humans but not by all other living humans. Some are shared by a few other living humans. What makes any one individual unique is the intersection of characteristics. You may, for example, be the *only* human at this moment with a mother from Mongolia and a father from Haiti, with an American nationality, with a Buddhist Jewish creed, who is left-handed with a dominant right foot, green eyes, a certain bald spot, lung cancer, aged 45, and male. That is a unique set of combined characteristics, but you also share any one of those characteristics with other people. For instance, you are not the only Buddhist Jew on planet earth.

The exhortation to think in terms of characteristics, not categories, contains a dilemma. The dilemma can be seen if we turn to linguistics. Adjectives can be thought of as being categorical (blond or brunette) or as existing along continua (very blond to very dark). But nouns are categorical. We might speak of the trans man or the cis man. But "man" is a category. It implies that there is another category of people who are not-man. But what if we think of a trans male person?

The focus on transgender experiences poses real challenges and presents real opportunities for those who see themselves as students or scholars in the area of gender research. At this time, we cannot predict where the conceptual paths will lead. But we can note two observations that hint at the future. First, by giving attention to transgender people, juxtaposing their inner lives with societal treatment, we are reminded of the work of pioneer feminist psychologists Rhoda Unger and Florence Denmark. Unger and Denmark (1975) urged researchers to look simultaneously at gender as the independent variable (subject) as well as the dependent variable (object) in any study. Second, we believe that the present focus in the academy on intersectionality is wholly consistent with our exhortation to think in terms of dimensions or characteristics rather than in terms of categories.

7.3 Concluding Wishes

In 2003, the Supreme Court of the United States handed down two decisions that permitted affirmative action to remain part of the admissions processes in universities, provided certain procedures were followed and certain other practices were avoided (Crosby, 2004). The heart of the winning argument was that all students, including white students as the majority ethnic group, benefitted by being in a student body that included and reflected the wider range of ethnic diversity in the US culture. This 2003 decision on affirmative action was about taking the continued steps to *truly integrate* US society from the 1960s into the present.

In a similar vein, we hope that this work will provide the majority gender experience, cis individuals, with the benefit of knowledge to truly integrate all experiences of gender into an understanding of society that reflects the true diversity of US culture. Like one of the authors, some readers may feel that that their increased knowledge about the experiences of trans individuals better equips them to be a good ally for someone in their life. In any case, all cis individuals who read this text have been presented with some pertinent and concrete information about their own experiences of gender, in addition to ones that might have been less available to them for whatever reason. Finally, we hope that a deeper understanding of what gender truly is – especially an understanding that it is not binary in any of its meanings – will help pave the way for the liberation of everyone.

References

Adams, K. A., Nagoshi, C. T., Filip-Crawford, G., Terrell, H. K., & Nagoshi, J. L. (2016). Components of gender-nonconformity prejudice. *International Journal of Transgenderism*, 17(3–4), 185–198. doi. https://doi.org/10.1080/15532739.2016.1200509

Aitken, M., Steensma, T. D., Blanchard, R., et al. (2015). Evidence for an altered sex ratio in clinic-referred adolescents with gender dysphoria. *Journal of Sexual Medicine*, 12(3), 756–763. doi: http://dx.doi.org.oca.ucsc.edu/10.1111/jsm.12817

Ames, J. (2005). *Sexual metamorphosis: An anthology of transsexual memoirs.* New York, NY: Vintage Books.

American Psychological Association. (2015). Guidelines for psychological practice with transgender and gender nonconforming people. *American Psychologist*, 70, 832–864. doi: http://dx.doi.org.oca.ucsc.edu/10.1037/a0039906

American Psychiatric Association. (2000). *Diagnostic and Statistical Manual of Mental Disorders-Text Revision*, (4th ed.). Washington, DC: Author.

American Psychiatric Association. (2016, Feb). *What is gender dysphoria?* https://www.psychiatry.org/patients-families/gender-dysphoria/what-is-gender-dysphoria

Amnesty International. (2016). *Sex workers at risk: A research summary of human rights abuses against sex workers.* www.amnestyusa.org/reports/sex-workers-at-risk-a-research-summary-of-human-rights-abuses-against-sex-workers/

Antoszewski, B., Kasielska, A., Jędrzejczak, M., & Kruk-Jeromin, J. (2007). Knowledge of and attitude toward transsexualism among college students. *Sexuality and Disability*, 25(1), 29–35. doi: https://doi.org/10.1007/s11195-006-9029-1

Arora, P. (2018, June 20). Poet Alok Vaid-Menon: "I am part of something greater than myself." *Huffington Post.* www.huffpost.com/entry/alok-vaid-menon_n_5b27dae4e4b0783ae12bd140

Badgett, M. V., Lau, H., Sears, B., & Ho, D. (2007). *Bias in the workplace: Consistent evidence of sexual orientation and gender identity discrimination.* https://williamsinstitute.law.ucla.edu/wp-content/uploads/Badgett-Sears-Lau-Ho-Bias-in-the-Workplace-Jun-2007.pdf

Baldner, C., & Pierro, A. (2019). The trials of women leaders in the workforce: How a need for cognitive closure can influence acceptance of harmful gender stereotypes. *Sex Roles*, 80, 565–577. https://doi.org/10.1007/s11199-018-0953-1

Balzer Carr, B., Ben Hagai, E., & Zurbriggen, E. L. (2017). Queering Bem: Theoretical intersections between Sandra Bem's scholarship and queer theory. *Sex Roles*, 76, 655–668. doi. /10.1007/s11199-015-0546-1

Bailey, J. M., & Zucker, K. J.(1995). Childhood sex-typed behavior and sexual orientation: A conceptual analysis and quantitative review. *Developmental Psychology*, 31, 43–55. doi: http://dx.doi.org.oca.ucsc.edu/10.1037/0012-1649.31.1.43

Baim, T. (2016, March 8). Second Wachowski filmmaker sibling comes out as trans. www.windycitymediagroup.com/lgbt/Second-Wachowski-filmmaker-sibling-comes-out-as-trans-/54509.html

Beatie, T. (2008). *Labor of love: The story of one man's extraordinary pregnancy*. New York, NY: Seal Press.

Bem, S. L. (1983). Gender schema theory and its implications for child development: Raising gender-aschematic children in a gender-schematic society. *Signs*, 8, 598–616. doi: http://dx.doi.org.oca.ucsc.edu/10.1086/493998

Bem, S. L. (1993). *The Lenses of Gender: Transforming the Debate on Sexual Inequality*. New Haven, CN: Yale University Press.

Bem, S. L. (1995). Dismantling gender polarization and compulsory heterosexuality: Should we turn the volume up or down? *Journal of Sex Research*, 32, 329–334. doi: 10.1080/00224499509551806

Berlinsky, D. L., & Specker, J. L. (1991). Changes in gonadal hormones during oocyte development in the striped bass, *Morone saxatilis*. *Fish Physiology and Biochemistry*, 9(1), 51–62.

Blackless, M., Charuvastra, A., Derryck, A., et al. (2000). How sexually dimorphic are we? Review and synthesis. *American Journal of Human Biology: The Official Journal of the Human Biology Association*, 12, 151–166.

Boedecker, A. L. (2011). *The transgender guidebook: Keys to successful transition*. New York, NY: CreateSpace Publishing.

Bono, C., & Fitzpatrick, B. (2011). *Transition: Becoming who I was always meant to be* [Kobo books]. www.kobo.com/us/en/ebook/transition–6

Brewster, M. E., Velez, B. L., Mennicke, A., & Tebbe, E. (2014). Voices from beyond: A thematic content analysis of transgender employees' workplace experiences. *Psychology of Sexual Orientation and Gender Diversity*, 1, 159–169. doi: http://dx.doi.org.oca.ucsc.edu/10.1037/sgd0000030

Broockman, D., & Kalla, J. (2016). Durably reducing transphobia: A field experiment on door-to-door canvassing. *Science*, 352, 220–224. doi: http://dx.doi.org.oca.ucsc.edu/10.1126/science.aad9713

Brown, G. R. (2010). Autocastration and autopenectomy as surgical self-treatment in incarcerated persons with gender identity disorder. *International Journal of Transgenderism*, 12, 31–39. doi: http://dx.doi.org.oca.ucsc.edu/10.1080 /15532731003688970

Brown, G. R. (2014). Qualitative analysis of transgender inmates' correspondence: Implications for departments of correction. *Journal of Correctional Health Care*, 20, 334–342. https://doi.org/10.1177/1078345814541533

Burke, M. (2011). Resisting Pathology: GID and the contested terrain of diagnosis in the transgender rights movement. In P. McGann, & D. Hutson (Ed.), *Sociology of Diagnosis: Advances in Medical Sociology*, (Vol. 12, pp. 183–210). Bingley: Emerald Group Publishing Limite.

Butler, J. (1990). *Gender Trouble: Feminism and the Subversion of Identity*. New York, NY: Routledge.

Byne, W., Bradley, S. J., Coleman, E. et al. (2012). Report of the American Psychiatric Association Task Force on Treatment of Gender Identity Disorder. *Arch Sex Behav* 41, 759–796. https://doi.org/10.1007/s10508-012-9975-x

Campbell, M., Hinton, J. D., & Anderson, J. R. (2019). A systematic review of the relationship between religion and attitudes toward transgender and gender-variant people. *International Journal of Transgenderism*, 20(1), 1–18. doi.org/10.1080/15532739.2018.1545149

Carpenter, L. F., & Marshall, R. B. (2017). Walking while trans: Profiling of transgender women by law enforcement, and the problem of proof. *William & Mary Journal of Women & Law*, 24, 5.

Cayne, C., & Jones, K. Z. (2017). *Hi gorgeous!* Philadelphia, PA: Running Press. www.kobo.com/us/en/ebook/hi-gorgeous–1

Cerankowski, K., & Milks, M. (2010). New orientations: Asexuality and its implications for theory and practice. *Feminist Studies*, 36, 650–664. http://www.jstor.org/stable/27919126

Ching, B.H., & Xu, J. T. (2018). The effects of gender neuroessentialism on transprejudice: An experimental study. *Sex Roles*, 78, 228–241. https://doi.org/10.1007/s11199-017-0786-3

Cohen, C. J. (1997). Punks, bulldaggers, and welfare Queens: The radical potential of queer politics? *GLQ: A Journal of Lesbian and Gay Studies*, 3, 437–465.

Cohen-Kettenis, P. T. (2005). Gender change in 46 XY persons with 5α-reductase-2 deficiency and 17β-hydroxysteroid dehydrogenase-3 deficiency. *Archives of Sexual Behavior*, 34, 399–410. doi. 10.1007/s10508-005-4339-4

Cohen-Kettenis, P. T., Mellenberg, G. J., Poll, N., Koppe, J. G., & Boer, K. (1999). Prenatal exposure to anticonvulsants and psychosexual development. *Archives of Sexual Behavior*, 28, 31–44.

Cohen-Kettenis, P., & Pfäfflin, F. (2010). The DSM diagnostic criteria for gender identity disorder in adolescents and adults. *Archives of Sexual Behavior*, 39, 499–513. doi: http://dx.doi.org.oca.ucsc.edu/10.1007/s10508-009-9562-y

Coleman, E., Bockting, W., Botzer, M. et al. (2012). Standards of care for the health of transsexual, transgender, and gender-nonconforming people, Version 7, *International Journal of Transgenderism*, 13(4), 165–232, doi: 10.1080/15532739.2011.700873

Coyote, I. V., & Spoon, R.(2014). *Gender failure*. Vancouver, Canada: Arsenal Pulp Press. www.kobo.com/us/en/ebook/gender-failure–4.

Crawford, M. E. (2006). *Transformations: Women, gender, and psychology*. New York, NY: McGraw-Hill.

Crawford, M., & Fox, A. (2007). IX. From sex to gender and back again: Co-optation of a feminist language reform. *Feminism & Psychology*, 17, 481–486. doi.org/10.1177/095935350708433.

Crosby, F. J. (2004). *Affirmative action is dead: Long live affirmative action*. New Haven, CT: Yale University Press.

Crosby, F. J., & Bearman, S. (2006). The uses of a good theory. *Journal of Social Issues*, 62, 413–437. doi: 10.1111k/154-/456-/2006/00458/x.

Crosby, F., & Wyche, K. F. (1996). Introduction: Coming together. In K. F. Wyche & F. Crosby (Eds.), *Women's ethnicities: Journeys through psychology* (pp. 1–4). Boulder, CO: Westview Press.

Cruz, C. (2011). LGBTQ street youth talk back: A meditation on resistance and witnessing. *International Journal of Qualitative Studies in Education*, 24, 547–558. doi: 10.1080/09518398.2011.600270

Davy, Z. (2010). Transsexual agents: Negotiating authenticity and embodiment within the UK's medicolegal system. In S. Hines & T. Sanger (Eds.), *Transgender identities: Towards a social analysis of gender diversity* (pp. 106–126). London, UK: Routledge.

Deaux, K., & Major, B. (1987). Putting gender into context: An interactive model of gender-related behavior. *Psychological Review*, 94(3), 369–389. https://doi.org/10.1037/0033-295X.94.3.369

Cox, L. (2019). *Laverne's story*. https://lavernecox.com/about/

Davy, Z. (2015). The DSM-5 and the politics of diagnosing transpeople. *Archives of Sexual Behavior*, 44, 1165–1176. doi./10.1007/s10508-015-0573-6

De Cuypere, G., Knudson, G., & Bockting, W. (2010). Response of the world professional association for transgender health to the proposed criteria for gender incongruence. *International Journal of Transgenderism*, 12, 119–123. doi/10.1080/15532739.2010.509214

Dessens, A. B., Slijper, F. M. E., & Drop, S. L. S. (2005). Gender dysphoria and gender change in chromosomal females with congenital adrenal hyperplasia. *Archives of Sexual Behavior*, 34, 389–397. doi: /10.1007/s10508-005-4338-5

Devor, A. H. (2004). Witnessing and mirroring: A fourteen-stage model of transsexual identity formation. *Journal of Gay & Lesbian Psychotherapy*, 8, 41–67.

Drescher, J. (2014). Controversies in gender diagnoses. *LGBT Health*, 1(1), 10–14. doi: /10.1089/lgbt.2013.1500

Drath, E. (Director)(2011). *Renée* [Film]. ESPN Films

Eagly, A. H. (2018). The shaping of science by ideology: How feminism inspired, led, and constrained scientific understanding of sex and gender. *Journal of Social Issues*, 74, 871–888. doi.org/10.1111/josi.12291

Egan, S. K., & Perry, D. G. (2001). Gender identity: A multidimensional analysis with implications for psychosocial adjustment. *Developmental Psychology*, 37, 451–463. doi./10.1037/0012–1649.37.4.451

Ehrensaft, D. (2011). *Gender born, gender made: Raising healthy gender-nonconforming children*. New York, NY: The experiment.

Ehrensaft, D. (2014). Listening and learning from gender-nonconforming children. *The Psychoanalytic Study of the Child*, 68, 28–56.

Ehrensaft, D. (2017). Gender nonconforming youth: current perspectives. *Adolescent Health, Medicine and Therapeutics*, 8, 57–67. doi.org/10.2147/AHMT.S110859

Elischberger, H. B., Glazier, J. J., Hill, E. D., & Verduzco-Baker, L. (2018). Attitudes toward and beliefs about transgender youth: A cross-cultural comparison between the United States and India. *Sex Roles*, 78, 142–160. https://doi.org/10.1007/s11199-017–0778-3

Factor, R., & Rothblum, E. (2008). Exploring gender identity and community among three groups of transgender individuals in the United States: MTFs, FTMs, and genderqueers. *Health Sociology Review*, 17, 235–253. doi: http://dx.doi.org.oca.ucsc.edu/10.5172/hesr.451.17.3.235

Faithful, R. (2009). Transitioning our prisons toward affirmative law: Examining the impact of gender classification policies on US transgender prisoners. *The Modern American*, 5, 3. https://digitalcommons.wcl.american.edu/tma/vol5/iss1/3/

Fausto-Sterling, A. (2019). Gender/sex, sexual orientation, and identity are in the body: How did they get there? *Journal of Sex Research*. doi: https://doi.org/10.1080/00224499.2019.1581883

Fast, A. A., & Olson, K. R. (2018). Gender development in transgender pre-school children. *Child Development*, 89, 620–637. doi: http://dx.doi.org.oca.ucsc.edu/10.1111/cdev.12758

Fiske, S. T., & Stevens, L. E. (1993). *What's so special about sex? Gender stereotyping and discrimination*. New York, NY; Sage Publications, Inc.

Flores, A. R. (2015). Attitudes toward transgender rights: Perceived knowledge and secondary interpersonal contact. *Politics, Groups, and Identities*, 3, 398–416. doi. /10.1080/21565503.2015.1050414

Flores, A., Miller, P., Tadlock. (2018). In J. K. Taylor, D. C. Lewis, & D. P. Haider-Markel (Eds.). *The remarkable rise of transgender rights* [Kobo books]. Ann Arbor, MI: University of Michigan Press. www.kobo.com/us/en/ebook/the-remarkable-rise-of-transgender-rights

Flores, A. R., Haider-Markel, D. P., Lewis, D. C., et al. (2018). Transgender prejudice reduction and opinions on transgender rights: Results from a mediation analysis on experimental data. *Research & Politics*, 5(1), 1–7. doi.org/10.1177/2053168018764945

Foucault, M. (1978). *The history of sexuality: An introduction*. Vol. 1. New York, NY: Vintage Books

Galupo, M. P., Pulice-Farrow, L., & Ramirez, J. L. (2019). "Like a constantly flowing river": Gender identity flexibility among non-binary transgender individuals. In J. D. Sinnott (Ed.), Identity flexibility during adulthood: Perspectives in adult development (pp. 163–177). New York, NY: Springer. http://dx.doi.org/10.1007/978-3-319-55658-1_10

Garelick, A. S., Filip-Crawford, G., Varley, A. H., et al. (2017). Beyond the binary: Exploring the role of ambiguity in biphobia and transphobia. *Journal of Bisexuality*, 17, 172–189. doi.org/10.1080/15299716.2017.1319890

Gillig, T. K., Rosenthal, E. L., Murphy, S. T., & Folb, K. L. (2017). More than a media moment: The influence of televised storylines on viewers' attitudes toward transgender people and policies. *Sex Roles*, 78, 515–527. doi: http://dx.doi.org.oca.ucsc.edu/10.1007/s11199-017-0816-1

Gilligan, C. (1982). *In a different voice*. Cambridge, MA: Harvard University Press.

Giordana, S. (2008). Lives in a chiaroscuro: Should we suspend the puberty of children with gender identity disorder? *Journal of Medical Ethics*, 34, 580–584. doi: 10.1136/jme.2007.021097

Glick, P., & Fiske, S. T. (1997). Hostile and benevolent sexism: Measuring ambivalent sexist attitudes toward women. *Psychology of Women Quarterly*, 21, 119–135.

Goldberg, A. E., & Kuvalanka, K. A. (2018). Navigating identity development and community belonging when "there are only two boxes to check": An exploratory study of nonbinary trans college students. *Journal of LGBT Youth*, 15, 106–131. https://doi.org/10.1080/19361653.2018.1429979

Goldberg, A. E., Kuvalanka, K. A., Budge, S. L., Benz, M. B., & Smith, J. Z. (2019). Health care experiences of transgender binary and nonbinary university students. *The Counseling Psychologist*, 47(1), 59–97. doi: http://dx.doi.org.oca.ucsc.edu/10.1177/0011000019827568

Grant, J. M., Mottet, L., Tanis, J. E., Harrison, J., Herman, J., & Keisling, M. (2011). *Injustice at every turn: A report of the national transgender discrimination survey*. National Center for Transgender Equality. www.transequality.org/sites/default/files/docs/resources/NTDS_Report.pdf

Gravholt, C., Juul, S., Naeraa, R., & Hansen, J. (1998). Morbidity in Turner Syndrome. *Journal of Clinical Epidemiology*, 51, 147–158.

Gray, J. (2009). *Men are from Mars, women are from Venus: Practical guide for improving communication*. Grand Rapids, MI: Zondervan.

Green, R. (1998). Mythological, historical, and cross-cultural aspects of transsexualism. In D. Denny (ed). *Current Concepts in Transgender Identity*, (2nd ed, Vol. 11, pp. 3–14). New York, NY: Garland Publishing.

Green, R., & Fleming, D. T. (1990). Transsexual surgery follow-up: Status in the 1990s. *Annual Review of Sex Research*, 1, 163–174.

Green, R. R., & Young, R. (2009). Hand preference, sexual preference, and transsexualism. *Archives of Sexual Behavior*, 30, 565–574.

Gurney, S., & Simmonds, J. (2007). Osteoporosis: a teenage perspective. *Physiotherapy*, 93, 267–272. doi.org/10.1016/j.physio.2006.12.004

Halberstam, J. (2017). *Trans*: A Quick and Quirky Account of Gender Variability*. Berkeley: University of California Press.

Hare, L., Bernard, P., Sanchez, E., et al. (2009). Androgen receptor repeat length polymorphism associated with male-to-female transsexualism. *Biological Psychology*, 65, 93–96.

Hylton, S., Gettleman, J., & Lyons, E. (2018, Feb 17). The peculiar position of India's third gender. www.nytimes.com/2018/02/17/style/india-third-gender-hijras-transgender.html

Harrison, B. F., & Michelson, M. R. (2019). Gender, masculinity threat, and support for transgender rights: An experimental study. *Sex Roles*, 80, 63–75. https://doi.org/10.1007/s11199-018-0916-6

Helgeson, V. (2016). *Psychology of gender*. London, UK: Routledge.

Hembree, W. C., Cohen-Kettenis, P., Delemarre-Van De Waal, H. A., et al. (2009). Endocrine treatment of transsexual persons: an Endocrine Society clinical practice guideline. *The Journal of Clinical Endocrinology & Metabolism*, 94, 3132–3154. https://doi.org/10.1210/jc.2009–0345.

Henley, N. (1977). *Body politics: Power, sex, and nonverbal communication.* Upper Saddle River, NJ: Prentice Hall.

Henley, N. M. (1995). Body politics revisited: What do we know today? In P. J. Kalbfleisch, & M. J. Cody (Eds.), *Gender, power, and communication in human relationships; gender, power, and communication in human relationships* (pp. 27–61). Hillsdale, NJ; Lawrence Erlbaum Associates, Inc.

Henningsson, S., Westerberg, L., Nilsson, S., et al. (2005). Sex steroid related genes and male to female transsexualism. *Psychoneuroendocrinology*, 30, 657–664.

Hines, M. (2005). *Brain gender.* Oxford, UK: Oxford University Press.

Hines, M., Brook, C., & Conway, G. S. (2004). Androgen and psychosexual development: Core gender identity, sexual orientation, and recalled childhood gender role behavior in women and men with congenital adrenal hyperplasia (CAH). *Journal of Sex Research*, 41, 75–81 doi. 10.1080/00224490409552215

Human Rights Campaign Staff. (2013 September 6). *Transgender workers at greater risk for unemployment and poverty.* www.hrc.org/blog/transgender-workers-at-greater-risk-for-unemployment-and-poverty

Hyde, J. S. (2005). The gender similarities hypothesis. *American Psychologist*, 60, 581–592.

Hyde, J. S., Bigler, R. S., Joel, D., Tate, C. C., & van Anders, S. M. (2019). The future of sex and gender in psychology: Five challenges to the gender binary. *American Psychologist*, 74, 171. doi.org/10.1037/amp0000307

Imperato-McGinley, J., Peterson, R. E., Gautier, T., & Sturla, E. (1979). Androgens and the evolution of male-gender identity among male pseudo-hermaphrodites with 5α-reductase deficiency. *New England Journal of Medicine*, 300, 1233–1237.

Ipsos, (2017 January 29). Global attitudes toward transgender people. www.ipsos.com/en-us/news-polls/global-attitudes-toward-transgender-people

James, S., Herman, J., Rankin, S., et al. (2016). *The report of the 2015 US transgender survey.* National Center for Transgender Equality [NCTE].www.transequality.org/sites/default/files/docs/USTS-Full-Report-FINAL.PDF

Jenner, C. (2015, 1 June). "I'm so happy after such a long struggle to be living my true self. Welcome to the world Caitlyn. Can't wait for you to get to know her/me" [Twitter Post]. twitter.com/caitlyn_jenner/status/605407919820013568?lang=en

Jenner, C., & Bissinger, B. (2017) *The secrets of my life* [Kobo Reader]. New York, NY: Grand Central Publishing. www.kobo.com/us/en/ebook/the-secrets-of-my-life–1

Jorgensen, C. (1967). *Christine Jorgensen: A personal biography.* New York, NY: Paul S. Eriksson, Inc.

Kamens, S. R. (2011). On the proposed sexual and gender identity diagnoses for DSM-5: History and controversies. *The Humanistic Psychologist*, 39, 37–59.

Katri, I. (2017). Transgender intrasectionality: Rethinking anti-discrimination law and litigation. *University of Pennsylvania Journal of Law and Social Change*, 20, 51. https://scholarship.law.upenn.edu/jlasc/vol20/iss1/4

Kattari, S. K., Whitfield, D. L., Walls, N. E., Langenderfer-Magruder, L., & Ramos, D. (2016). Policing gender through housing and employment discrimination: Comparison of discrimination experiences of transgender and cisgender LGBQ individuals. *Journal of the Society for Social Work and Research*, 7, 427–447. doi. https://doi.org/10.1086/686920

Keener, E., Mehta, C. M., & Smirles, K. E. (2017). Contextualizing Bem: The developmental social psychology of masculinity and femininity. In M.H. Kohlman & D. B. Krieg (Eds.)., *Discourses on gender and sexual inequality: The legacy of Sandra L. Bem* (Vol. 23, pp. 1–18). Bingley, UK: Emerald Publishing Limited.

Kleczkowska, A., Fryns, J.-P., & Van den Berghe, H. (1988). X-chromosome polysomy in the male. *Human Genetics*, 80, 16–22.

Kohlberg, L. (1966). A cognitive-developmental analysis of children's sex-role concepts and attitudes. In E. E. Maccoby (Ed.), *The development of sex differences* (pp. 82–173). Palo Alto, CA: Stanford University Press.

Kruijver, F., Zhou, J.-N., Pool, C. W., et al. (2000). Male to female transsexuals have female neuron numbers in a limbic nucleus. *Journal of Clinical Endocrinology and Metabolism*, 85, 2034–2041.

Kruse, R., Guttenbach, M., Schartmann, B., et al. (1998). Genetic counseling in patients with XXY/XXY/XY mosaic Klinefelter's syndrome: Estimates of sex chromosome aberrations in sperm before intracytoplasmic sperm injection. *Fertility and Sterility*, 69, 482–485.

Kuper, L. E., Nussbaum, R., & Mustanski, B. (2012). Exploring the diversity of gender and sexual orientation identities in an online sample of transgender individuals. *Journal of Sex Research*, 49, 244–254.

Kuvalanka, K. A., Bellis, C., Goldberg, A. E., & McGuire, J. K. (2019). An exploratory study of custody challenges experienced by affirming mothers of transgender and gender non-conforming children. *Family Court Review*, 57, 54–71.

Kuvalanka, K. A., Weiner, J. L., & Mahan, D. (2014). Child, family, and community transformations: Findings from interviews with mothers of transgender girls. *Journal of GLBT Family Studies*, 10, 354–379. doi: http://dx.doi.org.oca.ucsc.edu/10.1080/1550428X.2013.834529

Kuvalanka, K. A., Weiner, J. L., Munroe, C., Goldberg, A. E., & Gardner, M. (2017). Trans and gender-nonconforming children and their caregivers: Gender presentations, peer relations, and well-being at baseline. *Journal of Family Studies*, 31, 889–899.

Lambrese, J. (2010). Suppression of puberty in transgender children. *Virtual Mentor*, 12, 645–649. doi: 10.1001/virtualmentor.2010.12.8.jdsc1-1008

Landén, M., Innala, S. Attitudes Toward Transsexualism in a Swedish National Survey. *Arch Sex Behav* 29, 375–388 (2000). doi. https://doi.org/10.1023/A:1001970521182

Langowski, J., Berman, W. L., Holloway, R., & McGinn, C. (2017). Transcending prejudice: Gender identity and expression-based discrimination in the Metro Boston rental housing market. *Yale Journal of Law and Feminism*, 29, 321–371.

Leaper, C. (2000). Gender, affiliation, assertion, and the interactive context of parent–child play. *Developmental Psychology*, 36, 381–393. doi: http://dx.doi.org.oca.ucsc.edu/10.1037/0012-1649.36.3.381

Leaper, C., & Farkas, T. (2015). The socialization of gender during childhood and adolescence. In J. E. Grusec & P. D. Hastings (Eds.), *Handbook of socialization: Theory and research* (pp.541–565). New York, NY: Guilford Press.

Lee, J. (2015).*Coming out like a porn star: Essays on pornography, protection, and privacy.* Berkeley, CA; Stone Bridge Press.

Lees, P.(2019). Laverne Cox by Paris Lees. *The Queer Bible.* www.queerbible.com/queerbible/2017/9/21/laverne-cox

Lester Feder, J., Singer-Vine, J., & King, B. (2016, December 29). This is how 23 countries feel about transgender rights. Buzzfeed. www.buzzfeednews.com/article/lesterfeder/this-is-how-23-countries-feel-about-transgender-rights

Leszczynski, J. P., & Strough, J. (2008). The contextual specificity of masculinity and femininity in early adolescence. *Social Development*, 17, 719-736. doi: 10.1111/j.1467-9507.2007.00443.x

Lev, A. I. (2006). Disordering gender identity: Gender identity disorder in the DSM-IV-TR. *Journal of Psychology & Human Sexuality*, 17, 35–69.

Lev, A. I. (2013a). *Transgender emergence: Therapeutic guidelines for working with gender-variant people and their families.* New York, NY: Routledge.

Lev, A. I. (2013b). Gender dysphoria: Two steps forward, one step back. *Clinical Social Work Journal*, 41(3), 288–296. doi. https://doi.org/10.1007/s10615-013-0447-0

Liben, L. S., & Bigler, R. S. (2017). Understanding and undermining the development of gender dichotomies: The legacy of Sandra Lipsitz Bem. *Sex Roles*, 76, 544–555. doi.org/10.1007/s11199-015-0519-4

Lyons, T., Krüsi, A., Pierre, L., et al. (2016). Experiences of trans women and two-spirit persons accessing women-specific health and housing services in a downtown neighborhood of Vancouver, Canada. *LGBT Health*, 3, 373–378. doi: 10.1089/lgbt.2016.0060

Maccoby, E. E. (1990). Gender and relationships: A developmental account. *American Psychologist*, 45(4), 513–520.

Maccoby, E. E., & Jacklin, C. N. (1974). *The psychology of sex differences*. Palo Alto, CA: Stanford University Press.

Malkin, M. L., & DeJong, C. (2018). Protections for transgender inmates Under PREA: A comparison of state correctional policies in the United States. *Sexuality Research and Social Policy*, 1–15. https://doi.org/10.1007/s1317

Margolis, J. B. (2016). Two divorced parents, one transgender child, many voices. *Whittier Journal of Child and Family Advocacy*, 15, 125–164.

Martin, C. L., & Ruble, D. (2004). Children's search for gender cues: Cognitive perspectives on gender development. *Current Directions in Psychological Science*, 13, 67–70. doi: http://dx.doi.org.oca.ucsc.edu/10.1111/j.0963-7214.2004.00276.x

Martin, C. L., Ruble, D. N., & Szkrybalo, J. (2002). Cognitive theories of early gender development. *Psychological Bulletin*, 128(6), 903–933. doi: http://dx.doi.org.oca.ucsc.edu/10.1037/0033-2909.128.6.90

Martin, K. (1998). Becoming a gendered body: Practices of preschools. *American Sociological Review*, 63, 494–511.

Mazur, T. (2005). Gender dysphoria and gender change in androgen insensitivity or micropenis. *Archives of Sexual Behavior*, 34, 411–421. doi: http://dx.doi.org.oca.ucsc.edu/10.1007/s10508-005-4341-x

McGuire, J. K., Kuvalanka, K. A. Catalpa, J. M., & Toomey, R. B. (2016). Transfamily theory: How the presence of trans* family members informs gender development in families. *Journal of Family Theory & Review*, 8, 60–73. https://doi.org/10.1111/jftr.12125

Mehta, C. M. (2015). Gender in context: Considering variability in Wood and Eagly's traditions of gender identity. *Sex Roles*, 73, 490–496. doi.org/10.1007/s11199-015-0535-4

Mehta, C. M., & Dementieva, Y. (2017). The contextual specificity of gender: Femininity and masculinity in college students' same- and other-gender peer contexts. *Sex Roles*, 76, 604–614. https://doi.org/10.1007/s11199-016-0632-z

Meyerowitz, J. J. (2009). *How sex changed*. Cambridge, MA: Harvard University Press.

Michelraj, M. (2015). Historical evolution of transgender community in India. *Asian Review of Social Science*, 4, 17–9.

Miller, B. (2017). YouTube as educator: A content analysis of issues, themes, and the educational value of transgender-created online videos. *Social Media + Society*, 3(2), 2056305117716271. doi.org/10.1177/2056305117716271

Miller, P. R., Flores, A. R., Haider-Markel, D. P., et al. (2017). Transgender politics as body politics: Effects of disgust sensitivity and authoritarianism on transgender rights attitudes. *Politics, Groups, and Identities*, 5, 4–24. doi: 10.1080/21565503.2016.1260482

Mills, L. (2017, September 9). *Billy Tipton and the question of gender*. www.makingqueerhistory.com/articles/2017/9/8/billy-tipton-and-the-question-of-gender

Mizock, L., Hopwood, R., Casey, H., et al. (2017). The transgender awareness webinar: Reducing transphobia among undergraduates and mental health providers. *Journal of Gay & Lesbian Mental Health*, 21, 292–315. doi.org/10.1080/19359705.2017.1320696

Mock, J. (2014). *Redefining realness: My path to womanhood, identity, love and so much more*. New York, NY: Simon and Schuster.

Mock, J., & Mayo, K. (2011, May 8). I was born a boy. *Marie Claire*. www.marieclaire.com/sex-love/advice/a6075/born-male/

Morgan, T. (2007). Turner syndrome: Diagnosis and management. *American Family Physician*, 76, 405–417.

Morris, J. (2005). *Conundrum*. New York, NY: New York Review Classics.

Murakami, H. (2006). *Kafka on the Shore*. New York, NY: Vintage Books.

Nagoshi, J. L., Adams, K. A., Terrell, H. K., et al. (2008). Gender differences in correlates of homophobia and transphobia. *Sex Roles*, 59, 521–531. doi.org/10.1007/s11199-008-9458-7

Nealy, E. C. (2017). *Trans kids and teens: Pride, joy, and families in transition*. New York, NY: WW Norton & Company.

Nestle, J., Howell, C., & Wilchins, R. A. (2002). *Genderqueer: Voices from beyond the sexual binary*. New York, NY: Alyson Publications.

Nielsen, J., & Wohlert, M. (1991). Chromosome abnormalities found among 34910 newborn children: results from a 13-year incidence study in Aarhus, Denmark. *Human Genetics*, 87, 81–83.

Norton, A. T., & Herek, G. M. (2013). Heterosexuals' attitudes toward transgender people: Findings from a national probability sample of US Adults. *Sex Roles*, 68, 738–753. https://doi.org/10.1007/s11199-011-0110-6

Nygren, U., Södersten, M., Thyen, U., Köhler, B., & Nordenskjöld, A. (2019). On behalf of the DSD-LIFE Group: Voice dissatisfaction in individuals with a disorder of sex development. *Clin Endocrinol (Oxf)*. 91, 219–227. https://doi.org/10.1111/cen.14000

Olson, K. R. (2016). Prepubescent transgender children: What we do and do not know. *Journal of the American Academy of Child & Adolescent Psychiatry*, 55, 155–156. doi: http://dx.doi.org.oca.ucsc.edu/10.1016/j.jaac.2015.11.015

Olson, K. R., Durwood, L., DeMeules, M., & McLaughlin, K. A. (2016). Mental health of transgender children who are supported in their identities. *Pediatrics*, 137(3), e20153223.

Olson, K. R., & Enright, E. A. (2018). Do transgender children (gender) stereotype less than their peers and siblings? *Developmental Science*, 21(4), e12606. https://doi.org/10.1111/desc.12606

Olson, K. R., & Gülgöz, S. (2018). Early findings from the TransYouth Project: Gender development in transgender children. *Child Development Perspectives*, 12, 93–97.

Olson, K. R., Key, A. C., & Eaton, N. R. (2015). Gender cognition in transgender children. *Psychological Science*, 26, 467–474.

Pascoe, C. J. (2011). *Dude, you're a fag: Masculinity and sexuality in high school*. Berkeley, CA: University of California Press.

Perkiss, D. A. (2014). Boy or girl; Who gets to decide: Gender nonconforming children in child custody cases. *Hastings Women's Law Journal*, 25, 57–79.

Petrow, S. (2016, August 8). Do transgender athletes have an unfair advantage at the Olympics? www.washingtonpost.com/lifestyle/style/do-transgender-athletes-have-an-unfair-advantage-at-the-olympics/2016/08/05/08169676-5b50-11e6-9aee-8075993d73a2_story.html

Peterson, B. E., & Zurbriggen, E. L. (2010). Gender, sexuality, and the authoritarian personality. *Journal of Personality*, 78, 1801–1826. doi: 10.1111/j.1467-6494.2010.00670.

Pew (2017). About a third of Americans say society has gone too far in accepting transgender people. www.pewresearch.org/fact-tank/2017/11/08/transgender-issues-divide-republicans-and-democrats/ft_17-11-06_transgender_accepting/

Rametti, G., Carrillo, B., Gómez-Gil, E., et al. (2011a). White matter microstructure in female to male transsexuals before cross-sex hormonal treatment: A diffusion tensor imaging study. *Psychiatric Research*, 45, 199–204.

Rametti, G., Carrillo, B., Gómez-Gil, E., et al. (2011b). White matter microstructure in male to female transsexuals before cross-sex hormonal treatment: A DTI study. *Psychiatric Research*, 45, 949–954.

Raper, J. R. (1966). *Genetics of sexuality in higher fungi*. New York: Ronald Press.

Reiner, W. G., & Gearhart, J. P. (2004). Discordant sexual identity in some genetic males with cloacal exstrophy assigned to female sex at birth. *New England Journal of Medicine*, 350, 333–341.

Richards, R., & Ames, J. (1983). *Second serve: The Renee Richards story*. New York, NY: Stein & Day Pub.

Robnett, R. D. (2016). Gender bias in STEM fields: Variation in prevalence and links to STEM self-concept. *Psychology of Women Quarterly*, 40, 65–79. https://doi.org/10.1177/0361684315596162

Robles, R., Fresán, A., Vega-Ramírez, H., et al. (2016). Removing transgender identity from the classification of mental disorders: A Mexican field study for ICD-11. *The Lancet Psychiatry*, 3, 850–859. doi.org/10.1016/S2215-0366(16)30165-1

Rodemeyer, L. M. (2018) Feminist and transgender tensions: An inquiry into history, methodological paradigms, and embodiment. In C. Fischer, L. Dolezal (Eds.), *New feminist perspectives on embodiment: Breaking feminist waves* (pp. 103–123). New York: Palgrave Macmillan.

Rodriguez-Buritica, D. (2015). Overview of genetics of disorders of sexual development. *Current opinion in pediatrics*, 27(6), 675-684. doi.org/10.1097/MOP.0000000000000275

Rosenberg, R., & Oswin, N. (2015). Trans embodiment in carceral space: Hypermasculinity and the US prison industrial complex. *Gender, Place and Culture*, 22, 1269–1286.

Ruble, D. N., Taylor, L. J., Cyphers, L., et al. (2007). The role of gender constancy in early gender development. *Child Development*, 78, 1121–1136.

Trebay, G. (2008, June 22). He's Pregnant. You're Speechless. *New York Times*. www.nytimes.com/2008/06/22/fashion/22pregnant.html

Samons, S. L. (2009). Can this marriage be saved? Addressing male-to-female transgender issues in couples therapy. *Sexual and Relationship Therapy*, 24, 152–162. doi.org/10.1080/14681990903002748

Savin-Williams, R. C. (2009). *The new gay teenager* (Vol. 3). Cambridge, MA: Harvard University Press.

Savin-Williams, R.C., & Diamond, L. M. (2000). Sexual identity trajectories among sexual-minority youths: Gender comparisons. *Arch Sex Behav*, 29, 607–627. https://doi.org/10.1023/A:1002058505138

Serano, J. (2007). *Whipping girl: A transsexual woman on sexism and the scapegoating of femininity*. Berkeley, CA: Seal Press.

Serano, J. (2009, June 12). Psychology, sexualization and trans-invalidations. Keynote lecture presented at the 8th Annual Philadelphia

Trans-Health Conference. http://www.juliaserano.com/av/Serano-TransInvalidations.pd

Sevoliue, J., & Jenness, V, (2017). Challenges and opportunities for gender-affirming healthcare for transgender women in prison. *International Journal of Prisoner Health*, 13, 32–40. doi: 10.1108/IJPH-08-2016-0046

Shirdel-Havar, E., Steensma, T. D., Cohen-Kettenis, P. T., & Kreukels, B. P. (2019). Psychological symptoms and body image in individuals with gender dysphoria: A comparison between Iranian and Dutch clinics. *International Journal of Transgenderism*, 20(1), 108–117. doi. https://doi.org/10.1080/15532739.2018.1444529

Skougard, E. (2011). The best interests of transgender children. *Utah Law Review*, *2011*, 1161–1201.

Smith, D. (1998, June 2). One false note in a musician's life; Billy Tipton is remembered with love, even by those who were deceived. *New York Times*. www.nytimes.com/1998/06/02/arts/one-false-note-musician-s-life-billy-tipton-remembered-with-love-even-those-who.html

Smithers, G. D. (2014). Cherokee" two spirits": Gender, ritual, and spirituality in the native South. *Early American Studies: An Interdisciplinary Journal*, 12, 626–651.

Spack, N. P., Edwards-Leeper, L., Feldman, H. A. et al. (2012). Children and adolescents with gender identity disorder referred to a pediatric medical center. *Pediatrics*, 129(3), 418–425. doi: http://dx.doi.org.oca.ucsc.edu/10.1542/peds.2011-0907

Spade, D. (2003). Resisting medicine, re/modeling gender. *Berkeley Women's Law Journal* 18, 15.

Spence, J. T. (1993). Gender-related traits and gender ideology: Evidence for a multifactorial theory. *Journal of Personality and Social Psychology*, 64, 624–35.

Steensma, T. D., Biemond, R., de Boer, F., & Cohen-Kettenis, P. T. (2011). Desisting and persisting gender dysphoria after childhood: a qualitative follow-up study. *Clinical child psychology and psychiatry*, 16, 499–516. doi: /10.1177/1359104510378303

Steinmetz, K. (2014, May 29). The transgender tipping point. time.com/135480/transgender-tipping-point/

Stryker, S. (1999). Portrait of a transfag drag hag as a young man: The activist career of Louis G. Sullivan. In K. More, S. Whittle (Eds.), *Reclaiming genders: Transsexual grammars at the Ffin de siècle* (2nd ed, pp.62–82). London: Bloomsbury.

Stryker, S. (2008). *Transgender history*. New York, NY: Seal Press.

Stryker, S., & Silverman, V. (directors). (2005). *Screaming Queens: The Riot at Compton's Cafeteria* (film). San Francisco: Frameline Distributors.

Tadlock, B. L., Flores, A. R., Haider-Markel, D. P., et al. (2017). Testing contact theory and attitudes on transgender rights. *Public Opinion Quarterly*, 81, 956–972. doi: http://dx.doi.org.oca.ucsc.edu/10.1093/poq/nfx021

Tate, C. (2014). Gender identity as a personality process. In B. L. Miller (Ed.), *Gender identity: Disorders, developmental perspectives and social implications* (pp. 1–22). Hauppauge, NY: Nova.

Tate, C. C., Youssef, C. P., & Bettergarcia, J. N. (2014). Integrating the study of transgender spectrum and cisgender experiences of self-categorization from a personality perspective. *Review of General Psychology*, 18, 302–312. doi: http://dx.doi.org.oca.ucsc.edu/10.1037/gpr0000019

Taylor, J. K., Haider-Markel, D. P., & Lewis, D. C. (2018). *The remarkable rise of transgender rights*. Ann Arbor, MI: University of Michigan Press.

Tebbe, E. N., & Moradi, B. (2012). Anti-transgender prejudice: A structural equation model of associated constructs. *Journal of Counseling Psychology*, 59(2), 251–261. https://doi.org/10.1037/a0026990

Tee, N., & Hegarty, P. (2006). Predicting opposition to the civil rights of trans persons in the United Kingdom. *Journal of Community and Applied Social Psychology*, 16, 70–80. doi: http://dx.doi.org.oca.ucsc.edu/10.1002/casp.851

Teich, N. M. (2012). *Transgender 101: A simple guide to a complex issue*. New York, NY: Columbia University Press.

The Sylvia Rivera Law Project. (2007). It's war in here – Sylvia Rivera Law Project. https://srlp.org/files/warinhere.pdf

Thorne, B. (1993). *Gender play: Girls and boys in school*. London, UK: Rutgers University Press.

Transequality.org. (n.d). Housing and Homelessness. https://transequality.org/issues/housing-homelessness

Travers, A. (2018). *The trans generation: How trans kids (and their parents) are creating a gender revolution*. New York, NY: NYU Press.

Unger, R. K., & Denmark, F. L. (1975). *Woman: Dependent or independent variable?* New York, NY: Psychological Dimensions.

van de Grift, T. C., Pigot, G. L., Boudhan, S., et al. (2017). A longitudinal study of motivations before and psychosexual outcomes after genital gender-confirming surgery in transmen. *The Journal of Sexual Medicine*, 14, 1621–1628. doi.org/10.1016/j.jsxm.2017.10.064

Wachowski, L.(2012, Oct 24). Lana Wachowski's HRC visibility award acceptance speech (Transcript). *Hollywood Reporter.* www.hollywoodreporter.com /news/lana-wachowskis-hrc-visibility-award-382177

Wang-Jones, T. "Tie" S., Hauson, A. O., Ferdman, B. M., Hattrup, K., & Lowman, R. L. (2018). Comparing implicit and explicit attitudes of gay, straight, and non-monosexual groups toward transmen and transwomen. *International Journal of Transgenderism*, 19, 95–106. doi.org/10.1080 /15532739.2018.1428138

Warriner, K., Nagoshi, C. T., & Nagoshi, J. L. (2013). Correlates of homophobia, transphobia, and internalized homophobia in gay or lesbian and heterosexual samples. *Journal of Homosexuality*, 60, 1297–1314. doi: 10.1080/ 00918369.2013.806177.

Watjen, J., & Mitchell, R. W. (2013). College men's concerns about sharing dormitory space with a male-to-female transsexual. *Sexuality & Culture*, 17 (1), 132–166. doi. https://doi.org/10.1007/s12119-012-9143-4

West, C., & Zimmerman, D. H. (1987). Doing gender. *Gender and Society*, 1, 125–151.

Whitam, F. L., & Mathy, R. M. (1991). Childhood cross-gender behavior of homosexual females in Brazil, Peru, the Philippines, and the United States. *Archives of Sexual Behavior*, 20, 151–170.

Williams, C. (2014). Transgender. *Transgender Studies Quarterly*, 1, 232–234.

Winter, S., Webster, B., & Cheung, P. K. E. (2008). Measuring Hong Kong undergraduate students' attitudes towards trans people. *Sex Roles*, 59, 670–683. doi: /10.1007/s11199-008-9462-y

Wiepjes, C. M., Nota, N. M., de Blok, C. J., et al. (2018). The Amsterdam cohort of gender dysphoria study (1972–2015): trends in prevalence, treatment, and regrets. *The Journal of Sexual Medicine*, 15(4), 582–590. doi. https://doi.org /10.1016/j.jsxm.2018.01.016

Worrall, P. (2019 March 12). What is the row about transgender athletes all about? www.channel4.com/news/factcheck/factcheck-what-is-the-row-about-transgender-athletes-all-about

Worthen, M. G. (2016). Hetero-cis–normativity and the gendering of transphobia. *International Journal of Transgenderism*, 17(1), 31–57. doi. https://doi .org/10.1080/15532739.2016.1149538

Zhou, J.-N., Hofman, M.A., Gooren, L. J., & Swaab, D. F. (1995). A sex difference in the human brain and its relation to transsexuality. *Nature*, 378, 68–70.

Zucker, K. J. (2015). Evidence for an altered sex ratio in clinic-referred adolescents with gender dysphoria. Journal of Sexual Medicine, 12, 756–763. doi: http://dx.doi.org.oca.ucsc.edu/10.1111/jsm.128

Zucker, K. J. (2015). The DSM-5 diagnostic criteria for gender dysphoria. In C. Trombetta, G. Liguori and M. Bertolotto (Eds.), *Management of Gender Dysphoria* (pp. 33–37). Milan: Springer.

Zuloaga, D. G., Puts, D. A., Jordan, C. L., & Breedlove, S. M. (2008). The role of androgen receptors in the masculinization of brain and behavior: What we've learned from the testicular feminization mutation. *Hormones and Behavior*, 53, 613–626. doi: 10.1016/j.yhbeh.2008.01.013

Acknowledgments

The authors would like to thank Carole Allen, Rachelle Annechino, J. Blackwell, Susan Clayton, Zoey Kroll, Austin Richey-Allen and the anonymous reviewers for their helpful feedback on this manuscript. We would also like to thank Hillary Wilson for the images used in this manuscript.

About the Series
Many social psychologists have used their research to understand and address pressing social issues, from poverty and prejudice to work and health. Each Element in this series reviews a particular area of applied social psychology. Elements will also discuss applications of the research findings and describe directions for future study.

Cambridge Elements ⁼

Applied Social Psychology

Elements in the Series

Empathy and Concern with Negative Evaluation in Intergroup Relations:
Implications for Designing Effective Interventions
Jacquie D. Vorauer

The Psychology of Climate Change Adaptation
Anne van Valkengoed and Linda Steg

Undoing the Gender Binary
Charlotte Chucky Tate, Ella Ben Hagai and Faye J. Crosby

A full series listing is available at: www.cambridge.org/EASP

Printed in the United States
By Bookmasters